ALLIGATORS AND ME

Robert Rankin —
Keep those alligators domesticated and all will be well.

ALLIGATORS AND ME

MY LIFE IN ALABAMA 1968

a memoir

Molly Milner

Molly Milner

shoe button
PRESS

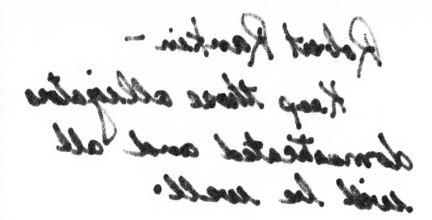

Published by Shoe Button Press, Los Angeles, California
mollymilner.com

Edited and Designed by Girl Friday Productions
www.girlfridayproductions.com

Editorial: Emilie Sandoz-Voyer, Michelle Hope Anderson, Wanda Zimba
Interior and Cover Design: Rachel Marek
Image Credits: © Patrick Jennings/Shutterstock; © nemlaza/Shutterstock

ISBN (Paperback): 978-0-9997692-0-1
e-ISBN: 978-0-9997692-1-8

First Edition

Printed in the United States of America

With loving thanks to—
My daughter, Megan Melissa Milner-Kutsch
My grandson, Corey Matthew Kutsch
And my husband and hero, Ned Milner

CONTENTS

TIMELINE

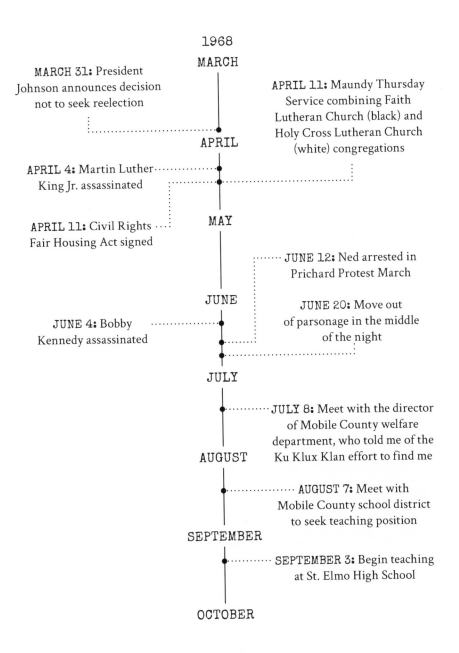

1968

MARCH

MARCH 31: President Johnson announces decision not to seek reelection

APRIL 11: Maundy Thursday Service combining Faith Lutheran Church (black) and Holy Cross Lutheran Church (white) congregations

APRIL

APRIL 4: Martin Luther King Jr. assassinated

APRIL 11: Civil Rights Fair Housing Act signed

MAY

JUNE 12: Ned arrested in Prichard Protest March

JUNE 20: Move out of parsonage in the middle of the night

JUNE

JUNE 4: Bobby Kennedy assassinated

JULY

JULY 8: Meet with the director of Mobile County welfare department, who told me of the Ku Klux Klan effort to find me

AUGUST

AUGUST 7: Meet with Mobile County school district to seek teaching position

SEPTEMBER

SEPTEMBER 3: Begin teaching at St. Elmo High School

OCTOBER

CHAPTER ONE

The Collar and the Call

Mobile? How had this happened to me? Mobile's somewhere in Alabama, isn't it? It never occurred to me that I would be traipsing off to the Deep South to live. I loved northern Ohio, magnificent Lake Erie, lush green summers, fall's beautiful colors, magical snowy winters. Most importantly, I cherished the wonderful close connections with my family, all of whom lived in this Ohio place . . .

Can't this decision be changed? Who are all these pompous, churchy, know-it-all men sitting around someplace—God knows where—making critical decisions for me . . . decisions like where my husband and I are going to live? This is more than my brain can handle!

Anxiously pacing back and forth in the living room of our small apartment in Springfield, Illinois, my husband and I began a heated discussion over what had occurred just a short time before, and I was railing over the upsetting news. We had returned from the long-awaited "Call ceremony" at seminary where each seminary graduate had been told where they would be sent to work after graduation. Some had been assigned to start up new churches, some had been assigned to open new foreign mission stations, and others had been assigned to pastor at existing congregations. And Ned's job offer had been to pastor a congregation in—of all places— Mobile, Alabama. What an incredible shock. Had they really said Mobile, Alabama?

Ned was dressed in his one and only suit with the requisite black clerical shirt underneath. I was always taken by the design of these black shirts. As a girl who had been around competent seam-stresses all my life, I was struck with the notion that these cleri-cal shirts were patterned so that the buttons were hidden. Where you would normally see buttons lined up down the front of an ordinary white shirt, there was instead on clerical black shirts a well-tailored fold laid over the plebeian black buttons, as if seeing the rude little disks would distract from *the man of God* image that came with the person wearing this shirt.

Topping the black shirt and attached by a few discreet little metal studs, was the stiff, hospital-white plastic clerical collar. The whole presentation—black shirt, white collar—made a definitive statement. To me it said, *I am the real thing, you know. God and I are on best terms, an* this outfit vali*ates it.*

I loved how handsome Ned looked in this garb. I suppose I took the same sort of pride when he wore it as a military wife feels when the dress uniform is buttoned up on her special per-son. This carefully prescribed formal attire that clergy wear in some mainline denominations had always been denigrated in my Baptist upbringing, however. But now, married to a man who wore clerical clothes regularly, I found the whole look quite appealing. For me it seemed to add a level of genuine authenticity to the whole idea of a clergyman. What I never really understood, though, was how that stiff little white collar held some mysteri-ous power over me.

So as our tense discussion about the new assignment to Mobile grew louder, it almost seemed as though my husband's clerical garb was a third person in the room. Inside my head, I knew the tentative plan after seminary graduation. The seminary hierarchy would assign Ned to a pastoral type job somewhere or another. The God-fearing Lutheran seminary hierarchy liked to frame this assignment as "the Call." This terminology was designed to keep the whole assignment process religiously correct as far as the Lutheran subculture was concerned. In defining each new job offer as a "Call from God," the otherwise ordinary and mundane process of assigning people to jobs was slathered in heavy-duty religious sauce—one that few people in the church world would ever challenge. Over time, the hugely significant "Call from God" term was shortened simply to "the Call."

When I would think about this term, the Call, I'd visualize it as if the true voice from God came straight out of heaven and sped through space, skipping over every set of ears in the world to go directly into those of the seminary guys. And there it would stop. These religious power brokers then had their directions. They knew without a shadow of a doubt which graduate to send where— no other discussion was needed because of their direct pipeline to God. Well, maybe God's voice does work this way, I don't know. But right now, standing in the living room of our comfy apartment over the dentist's office in Springfield, what I learned about the Call process sounded suspicious, especially to my newly forming women's lib ears.

The Call thing worked this way for Ned. Holy Cross Lutheran Church in Mobile, one of several Lutheran congregations across the country, had found itself without a pastor when the former one moved on to another congregation. Holy Cross formally made a request to the Lutheran seminary for a new graduate to take over the job. The seminary men in charge looked over this request application, along with a whole slew of similar requests. Then with God's voice in their ears directing them, they assigned Ned to Holy Cross Lutheran Church in Mobile.

The process provided an organized way to find job placements for most new seminary graduates under cover of an official God-ordained umbrella. To their credit, seminary gurus conducted a brief interview with each of the seminary grads before assignments were made. But at least in Ned's case, no recognition is given to his expressly requested job placement choice: an inner-city congregation. It would seem that God (with the help of seminary men) had other things in mind for Ned.

Although the seminary faculty had at least taken a few moments to talk with my eager husband about the job-placement possibilities before the actual assignment was given, no one ever, including Ned, had talked with me about the location of Ned's new assignment, which just happened to be the location of my new home, too. Women in this Lutheran bubble, as in most Christian circles, were pretty much considered incidental baggage.

To that very matter, in spring of Ned's final year of seminary, a meeting was organized for the future pastors' wives by a couple of enthusiastic seminary professors (all men). We were told how blessed we were to be married to potential Lutheran pastors. We were told how it was our job to be dutiful, obedient wives, and just as importantly, generous and self-sacrificing "First Ladies of the Parsonage." These stodgy males made it clear that our primary responsibility as compliant clergy wives was to produce little Lutheran children and raise them in the tenets of the faith. "Children are God's gifts, and you are to bring forth as many as you can," they said. The message was unequivocal.

I had been raised a fundamentalist Baptist. And much of the Lutheran version of what a minister's wife was all about I had already witnessed growing up. But since I had attended a non-fundamentalist college, I had become more and more influenced by the heady ideals of the newly burgeoning women's liberation movement. I listened to Gloria Steinem and began to consider the possibility that I had a right to my own self-determination even though I happened to be born female. What a stunning concept for me. Betty Friedan's book *The Feminine Mystique* held a prominent place in my thinking as I was attempting to integrate my rigid religious dictates of what a woman should be with the intoxicating ideas of women's lib.

I became haunted by a particularly poignant quote of Friedan's: "It is easier to live through someone else than to become complete yourself." I found the words unsettling. This lofty goal of completing myself kept dancing elusively in front of me. But I felt I was in a dead-end situation. I had willingly taken on the job as wife of a religious man, and my husband's superiors had told me how I should live that life. Unfortunately, the job description of the perfect pastor's wife appeared to exclude the task of learning how to complete myself.

So what stuck in my craw on that memorable night of the Call was the notion that the decision-making procedure involved little collaboration with the seminary graduate and absolutely no involvement with the wife. Not that my input as a wife should have been the final word, no. But it would have been wonderful to know someone thought I was worth listening to. Just being allowed to be part of the discussion would have been nice. But no such considerations had been shown.

I struck out at Ned again, asking, "Who do they think they are? How arrogant of these men to sit around and make decisions for me as though I don't even exist. I feel as if I have no value at all." And then I continued, "This whole bunch of Lutheran know-it-all men should be hung at dawn."

I aimed my anger next specifically at Ned, who was growing more upset by the minute. I quipped, "Why didn't you have more say in all this?" All this was the religious structure that just happened to be my husband's choice as the foundation of his new career. He felt threatened having to defend the system he had chosen to become a part of. It would seem empathy and patience were fine characteristics for a clergyman to model for others, but not when one's own wife pushed her agenda too far.

Ned's face pulled up into a rather threatening grimace. He responded, "Why can't you be more loyal to what I want? I've decided I like the Call to Mobile. I think it's a pretty good assignment, all things considered." And then as he stomped out of the room in a cloud of defiance, he lashed out sarcastically, "Sorry you don't like it."

It's important to bring this whole job-assignment thing into focus. It had never occurred to me that the Call for my husband would be somewhere far from my family and the place where I grew up and still wanted to live. What a naive ninny I was. I had somehow expected my husband would have spoken up on my behalf during his assignment interview. But in the immature fog of our early relationship, I hadn't even discussed the matter with him. Then I learned something particularly shocking: my husband didn't see my interests as having any value in this seminary assignment stuff anyway. He considered the matter to be about his life only, not mine, even though I was legitimately married to the man. The point is, nobody—my husband included—much cared about my thoughts on where I would be living. I was expected to just go silently along as all good wives did, especially in religious bubbles.

But you see, I had my life all planned differently. My dreams were quite concrete. I never really discussed these dreams with Ned but foolishly assumed he could read my mind, I guess. I thought he knew exactly what I wanted. And absurdly, I believed that what I wanted, he wanted, too. I wanted to live somewhere close to my family and have an idyllic life as the wife of a respected pastor. I dreamed I might even become a version of Miss Goody Two-Shoes, adored by her husband and loved by the congregation. It seemed like a wonderfully saccharine-sweet plan at the time. I delighted in what the future might hold as the wife of a brilliant, promising minister in a mainline Christian tradition. I believed by marrying Ned I had found an honorable purpose for my life. If things worked out well, I might even have the added opportunity to become a woman of some repute as a spiritual speaker or writer for women's groups. The whole dream was a bit heady, but woefully shallow and immature, to say the least.

What I didn't realize, though, in marrying Ned was that these adolescent dreams would soon be rudely replaced by another agenda, one that in its ferociousness would shake my life to the core. Nothing, and I mean nothing, turned out as I had thought it would.

...

Ned had come from German Mennonite stock with an immigrant grandfather who, long before either of us were born, had been a hired hand on my grandfather's large farm in Wellington, Ohio. Loose family connections bolstered by similar religious persuasions had continued between our two families for over four decades. An aunt of Ned's had formally introduced us in 1964. He and I began exchanging letters—me a student at Baldwin–Wallace College in Berea, Ohio, and Ned a seminarian in Springfield, Illinois. Within a few months, he was sent to intern at an inner-city congregation in Detroit. By then I had graduated and was teaching English to middle school kids in Cleveland, and our long-distance romance began.

It didn't take me long to become captivated by Ned's energetic commitment to liberal causes. Very quickly Ned became my hero—my Prince Charming. Quite revolutionary to me was his radical devotion to social justice, inspired by Christian precepts. Frankly, this drew me to him even though his rhetoric was in direct opposition to the fundamentalist religious worldview in which I had been raised. Ned brought to our relationship a variety of world experiences—the United States Coast Guard Academy, Colorado School of Mines, Army Security Agency in Okinawa, and now Lutheran seminary. I found the depth, maturity, and insight he displayed head and shoulders over other men I'd dated. And his willingness to examine his faith with a no-holds-barred approach—at one point even abandoning it for a while—sealed my respect for the authenticity of his belief system. Before long I knew without a doubt he was the man I wanted to marry.

A conservative fundamentalist Christian family and church had been my whole life growing up. My parents, grandparents, and most all the relatives I had contact with were of the same Baptist religious brand. We all ate, slept, lived, and celebrated believing we were really God's chosen folks. We knew we were the only people who had the straight scoop from the Almighty because we believed we had dutifully followed the "prescribed" biblical plan to reach that elusive place of salvation.

We believed God thought we were pretty special—pretty lovable—because of what we had done to get saved. This inside connection with God gave us the right to sit in judgment of any other belief system, even other Christian groups . . . especially other Christian groups. As long as you stayed within the fundamentalist Baptist prescribed lists of dos and don'ts in your life, you were on safe ground. It was easy for me to learn the requirements of this system and not hard to live within the safe zone, as long as my friends and inspirational contacts were drinking the same Kool-Aid. But step outside the fortress that protected all the right beliefs and you'd run afoul of the system. Although I can't remember *wanting* to intentionally step outside, unfortunately for my family, I certainly did.

Growing up, I was secure and happy in this reactionary bubble. I saw the people I worshiped with as my extended family. I felt as though I belonged to a loving, nurturing crowd, all of whom shared common religious beliefs. It felt good to be a member of a group who continually congratulated each other for knowing what the right belief system was and lived accordingly.

But as I grew older, occasionally unsettling curiosities rose up within me. I don't remember that these curious feelings had anything to do with a sense of rebellion. Rather when these feelings did occur, it seemed they were encouraging me to only briefly step out of the system bubble. I wanted to find out what the outside world was really all about, that's all. I took on religiously unauthorized activities like attending Pete Seeger or Joan Baez concerts at Oberlin College. And I started attending Saturday-night services at a synagogue with my Jewish friend, Carole.

These "outside the bubble" activities unnerved my father to no end, and he blustered around the house, ranting about the incorrectness of it all. He carried on angrily about how I should never even think about converting to Judaism: after all, I was fundamentalist Christian. Further, didn't I know how Pete Seeger and Joan Baez were Communists (which was a code name for satanists.)

The summer after I graduated high school, the 1960 presidential campaign was in full swing. My right-wing family's candidate choice was, of course, Richard M. Nixon. While keeping up with the presidential campaign news, I noticed that young, handsome John Fitzgerald Kennedy, that pope-worshiping (according to my father) Catholic Democrat candidate, was coming to our town as part of his Ohio tour. Curiosity prompted me to discover that after JFK's brief speech in the downtown square, his entourage would probably be driving by our house on the way to the little local airport. I donned a pair of cutoff jeans with a fresh blue-and-white-striped cotton blouse. With my hair pulled back in a tight ponytail, I went out on the front porch. Bouncing down the stoop, I perched myself casually on the bottom front step in the warm summer sun to wait.

My house sat on a main thoroughfare in town, Middle Ave. It was a divided street running north–south for about sixteen blocks or so from what at one time had been the outskirts of town to the main downtown square. The divider in the middle was a prominent stretch of grass about five feet wide that ran the length of the sixteen blocks. As I sat there on the stoop, my eyes became glued to the two lanes on the opposite side of the street coming from downtown. I didn't know if my calculations were on target, but I figured if I were right, JFK's entourage would come along any minute.

I didn't have to wait long before a group of three impressive-looking cars appeared on the opposite side of the street. And before I knew it, I saw a wonderful, classy black Lincoln convertible. The top was down. None other than John Fitzgerald Kennedy himself, dressed in a snazzy dark-blue suit, a white shirt, and a tie, sat in the back on the folded-down top, his feet resting on the back seat. About a block before the car was in front of me, I started to eagerly wave. It's still hard for me to believe, but JFK did indeed look over at me, and I believe our eyes connected. With his terrific charismatic smile plastered across his handsomely tanned face, he raised his arm and actually waved back at me for a bit. There was no one else on the street in either direction, so I knew I was registering in his line of vision, and I was thrilled.

"Thrilled" is not the word I would use to describe my family's reaction when I went inside and excitedly told them what had just happened. "Disgusted" and "horrified" might be better word choices. My father started his ranting again about JFK, the pope-loving radical, who if elected would, among other diabolic things, move the White House to the Vatican. And besides, why would I ever want to waste my time sitting on the front steps to watch this no-good Democrat go by?

Well, that's a small picture of where I had come from when I chose to marry an aspiring young Lutheran minister with radical leanings. My fundamentalist father was not happy about the Lutheran part at all, as it did not fit the religious side of life he had in mind for me. After all, Lutherans were not of a mind to require folks to demonstrate the validity of their religious belief by marching down the center aisle of church publicly professing their faith, like my Baptist family believed. And I never discussed Ned's liberal leanings with my dad, ever, so he was unaware of this ticking time bomb before my marriage.

In trying to explain the religious differences to my father, I claimed that Lutherans were more or less a catholic-lite experience, the "lite" part meaning, of course, no pope. I thought the no-pope part would promote the authenticity of Lutherans to my father. I went on to tell him that Martin Luther, the man for whom the group was named, had lived his whole life with a laser focus on the then-radical concept of justification by faith, not works. And Luther's courageous efforts had been the driving force behind the Protestant Reformation.

My father responded with the irrefutable comment that *our* Baptist religious group had not needed the Protestant Reformation to part ways with the Catholic church anyway. We had never been a part of the Catholic faith, ever. He told me he knew, without question, that our thread of believers had always met together in small groups apart from the Catholics, holding the same correct tenets learned directly from Jesus himself. And these basic faith precepts continued unchanged—all these centuries later. We were absolutely pure, unadulterated Christians from the very beginning with Jesus—never contaminated by Catholics or any other false beliefs. How could you get any more religiously right-thinking than that?

I was lucky, though. At least my family cared enough about me to continue listening despite my flirtation with "worldly ways"—as they loosely defined any actions outside the fundamentalist bubble. But there was one sticking point my father kept bringing up, and that was the issue of well-educated clergy. My dad was correct that there was a formal, advanced-education requirement for clergy in the Lutheran faith tradition. My father was sure this prerequisite opened the door for inappropriate questioning among authentic "believers."

My dad's opinion was that religious beliefs regarding God and the Bible given to him by his trusted church should never be questioned. He was certain that radical religious concepts always emanated from educated clergy. This issue seemed to my dad, then, to be a very good reason to reject my choice of an educated Lutheran minister as a future husband.

Now, let me be clear, I was also not completely on board with the differences between my fundamentalist Baptist upbringing and the tenants of Lutheranism. The Lutheran ideas of liturgy, infant baptism, and the Eucharist were, without question, bumps in the road for me. But as far as I could see, this Lutheran belief system was strongly grounded in biblical writings and was founded on essentially the same basic faith I already held.

And, beyond all else, I was in love. It was clear to me that my brilliant future husband, who had himself been raised fundamentalist Baptist, had weighed all the components of these conflicting thoughts. And after much soul-searching, Ned had authentically settled on Lutheranism. So without a doubt, I was confident I could work out the details as long as I was with him. Love held a compelling optimism for me.

Ned had been very romantic and kind in courting me, and I was sure that my feelings for him were genuine. My family found much to disagree with religiously in my choice of a mate, but the long history of family connections back to our grandfathers' time did help to override the negativity. Thankfully, bigotry is sometimes diluted by personal relationships between the bigot and the target. So my father eventually cared enough for me to get to know Ned better and then finally go along with my choice. Ned and I were married in his Lutheran church the day after Christmas in 1965.

In January, I left my job in the Cleveland public schools and went to Springfield, Illinois, to live with my new husband. Ned was finishing his last semester of Lutheran seminary, and in Springfield, I taught middle school English. It was at this crossroads in our new married existence that I learned of Ned's Call to Holy Cross Lutheran Church in Mobile.

•••

In our Springfield apartment, a bit of time had elapsed after his dramatic exit. When he returned to the living room, our heated discussion continued. My husband was quite ill-tempered about the fact that I wouldn't go merrily along with the Mobile news. Ned told me I should be happy for him. He said after he thought about the situation for a bit, he believed he had received "a good Call." My words had come across as attacking him personally. And maybe I had been when I asked if he had ever thought about my wishes in any of this. He hadn't, of course, and this matter was not something he wanted to talk any more about. He clearly stated, "This is my business, not yours, after all."

Ned did listen to me carry on for a while longer, however, until I wore myself down. The air was heavy with hurt feelings on both sides. But hanging in the silence at the end of my rant was the unspoken knowing between us that I would—sometime soon—give in to the overriding expectations of my husband's career needs. I would eventually go along, as cheerfully as possible, to Alabama. Ned had learned early on in our relationship that after reflection I usually found myself in an uncomfortable place. It was no surprise, then, that at the end of the evening, I found myself in a concoction of my own making: guilt soup.

My guilt soup came together seasoned with thoughts about how a good wife should get over herself and move on with what was best for her husband. For me, that man was the one who wore the clerical collar—God's man on earth. For my entire life, I had soaked up basic cultural and religious tenets of what it meant to be a good wife, and my flirtations with women's lib ideals were new and untested. The Mobile move seemed to be what was best for my husband, so I began to believe it was what was best for me, too. The notion of completing myself seemed, after all, little more than sheer selfishness.

So after Ned's graduation from seminary, we returned to the Cleveland area to pack our belongings for our move south. Languid summer days provided a chance for me to rethink making Mobile my new home. Time was beginning to give me perspective on this relocation, an idea I had at first rejected completely. I began to read all I could about Mobile. To my surprise, I found myself becoming a bit charmed by the prospect of living there.

Being a committed new bride of a budding radical activist also helped me come around. Ned was now putting a super shine on his great attitude about the prospects Mobile offered him. He was excited for the opportunity to work in the Deep South where civil rights issues continued to be major news every day. And if he was excited, I was content. My 1950s attitude was all about being the devoted wife. And I knew that, without question, the devoted wife made life good by buying into whatever made the man in her life happy, especially if he wore a clergy collar.

CHAPTER TWO

Mobile at Last

With our belongings carefully tucked into the car, we started the two-day trip south to Mobile. Crossing the Alabama state line on day two, I saw flat open spaces scattered with southern yellow pine and low, scratchy scrubs. We crossed long, well-established, sturdy bridges with names sounding like they came right from a Faulkner novel: Tombigbee Waterway, Spanish River, and Chacaloochee Bay. I grew more curious as each new sign marker passed the window. Ned's excitement was clearly noticeable, too. He slid his hands back and forth around the steering wheel singing snippets from "Ol' Man River." Good-humoredly, he told me he was getting into the habit of expressing himself in a more Southern, gentile way. The promise of a happy future for us in this new place was becoming palpable.

Finally, in the early evening, we reached Mobile. I looked over at Ned, who was brimming with satisfaction. He radiated a delighted smile that gave his large brown eyes a rascal-like crinkle. As we turned west onto Government Street, I became swallowed up in a lovely, dreamlike scene. Beautifully laced limbs of gigantic live oak trees canopied over each side of the street. Majestic branches dripping with long tendrils of Spanish moss created a sense of otherworldliness. Antebellum mansions, impressive historic buildings, and old churches peeped out between intertwining leaves. The air, heavy with humidity, was saturated with a strange, sweet, almost intoxicating flower fragrance. Twilight surrounded us. Everything seemed to be conspiring to create an extraordinary welcome. How lucky I felt. The two of us together at that moment were overtaken with a certainty that we were on the threshold of a wonderful new life. But neither of us had a clue as to the challenges this new life would eventually bring us.

A few miles farther, we found ourselves in the comfortable middle-class community of Cottage Hill. It was clearly "new" Mobile, as opposed to the enchanting historic downtown section. The 1950s cookie-cutter ranch-style homes were scattered helter-skelter along gently curving roads. Each redbrick house, with an almost fragile-looking carport clinging tightly to one side, was nicely situated back from the street. Lots were generously sized.

As Ned turned the car onto Merritt Drive, our new house appeared. Since my attitude about living in Mobile had completely reversed itself, I felt a little like it was Christmas morning. It was our first official home as pastor and pastor's wife. I could hardly wait for this new chapter of my life to get underway. I had such splendid thoughts of what this existence would be like, and I felt so delighted to be married to this terrific man.

The parsonage was part of the compensation package offered to Ned as pastor of Holy Cross Lutheran Church. As was the usual arrangement with pastors, the parsonage came unfurnished. Shipped from Ohio, and arriving before us, were a bedroom set gifted me from my grandparents on my high school graduation; an antique drugstore table and chair set from a New England vacation; an odd assortment of cast-off chairs and small tables from my family; and a grand, antique oak, leather-top desk Ned and I had happily acquired in Springfield. We had fantasized that this enormous piece had possibly once belonged to Abraham Lincoln, since we were living in Lincoln country when we'd bought it, and so we treated it with a ridiculous sense of awe. Aside from the car, this motley collection of furniture was pretty much the sum and substance of our external belongings. The approximately one-thousand-square-foot parsonage included a living/dining area, a kitchen, two bedrooms, a small den, and a bath, with an attached carport. The whole package, tailor-made for our new life here, was just perfect for our bits and pieces.

We were grateful to see that congregation members had graciously unpacked boxes before our arrival. In thoughtfulness, church volunteers had cleaned the parsonage and generously left fresh grocery items—milk, butter, bacon, eggs, and orange juice—cooling in the on-loan refrigerator. I was especially impressed with a loaf of homemade sour cream pound cake wrapped tightly in foil. Later I found out Mrs. Monk, a congregation member, had baked the delicious gift. It should be no surprise that even these forty-five years later, I still bake Mrs. Monk's wonderful sour cream pound cake for special occasions. It always brings back memories of our first fantastic day in Mobile.

Later that same evening, I realized there was one disconcerting piece to the otherwise engaging picture. It was a strange, noxious odor. Focusing on its presence took some time, but once I did, I couldn't get it out of my thoughts. I realized how the essence was aggressively creeping into my nose, mouth, eyes, and even brain. There was no way to stop it. The strange, sweet flower fragrance from downtown Mobile had been replaced with this odd, caustically offensive, and overwhelmingly distracting smell.

Joe, a church volunteer who was helping us get settled, told me this perverse irritant was the stench of sulfur dioxide given off by a whole collection of International Paper mills as a by-product in the process of bleaching paper items. He followed with the fact that paper mills were the bedrock of the Mobile economy, so people didn't really want to find too much fault with the smell. So the all-to-frequent disgusting odor was an unpleasant state of affairs I quickly learned to live with, like it or not.

The absurd irony of this situation was that Ned had been born without a sense of smell, a condition inherited from his dad. So while I eventually had to contend with a frequent annoying diversion in the air—the foul odor of sulfur dioxide—it never disturbed Ned's psyche one bit. It would seem this situation mirrored other circumstances in our lives—things that I found difficult to deal with that never even fazed my husband, like the pervasive fear I felt from Klan threats later, which had surprisingly little effect on him.

And so we started our life in this new place, full of excitement and anticipation, with no idea whatsoever what a year or two would bring our way.

CHAPTER THREE

The Tempest

Ned hunkered down at work wanting to show everyone what a super-dedicated pastor he could be. He was fired up. Exciting hard work was not new to Ned. As a cadet at the United States Coast Guard Academy, he'd been aboard the tall ship, the *Eagle*, on two summer cruises. One of the perks of this endeavor was meeting Ernest Hemingway in Cuba. Transferring after two years to the Colorado School of Mines, he ended up in a job working as a geophysical engineer looking for oil on the Navajo Indian Reservation. Then, with his draft number coming up, Ned had voluntarily joined the military and become an Army specialist in Okinawa operating IBM machines trying to break secret codes.

It was in the independent winds of this Japanese island that my soul-searching spouse-to-be had found a sense of renewed connection with God. After a dark-night-of-the-soul period where he'd lost his faith altogether, Ned had taken a one-hundred-eighty-degree turn and had decided—without a shadow of a doubt—to return to his teenage dream of becoming a Christian minister after his military service. So, to be clear, Ned was not inexperienced in the world of work or in matters of faith when he arrived as a Lutheran pastor in Mobile in 1966.

In the first few months, my husband's sermons became more and more engaging, and much of his time was spent with congregation members in crisis. Ned began to see the beginnings of a devoted following in his new congregation. In fact, one enthusiastic church member, Bryan Short, was so taken with Ned's preaching skills, he wanted to nominate Ned as a potential guest speaker for *The Lutheran Hour*, a weekly national radio show. Ned was flattered but did not accept the honor. He was too focused making a name for himself at Holy Cross Lutheran Church.

But Ned's supersize career efforts had a downside in our marriage. In no time at all, I learned what it felt like to be left home alone for very long periods of time. Before I realized it, homesickness began to play a big role in my life.

Underneath it all, Ned seemed to feel he was one of the saintly few who really got it—who truly cared about the important issues in life. This premise was never put into words, but the overall message was clear nonetheless. Ned appeared to consider his energy of value only when spent on what he considered to be noble activities.

But the obsessive moral commitment that fueled him never seemed to have enough space to include me. I felt left out and neglected. I often sensed he perceived me as a source of negative energy just getting in his way.

In my melancholy, I forgot—or, more to the point, *ignored*—the fact that I had willingly agreed to come to Mobile. I had the reoccurring thought that Ned should overlook my decision to move so far away from my family and simply make everything right by packing me up and taking me back to Ohio. But I didn't have the internal fortitude to tell him this selfish dribble. So I just allowed the poison to fester inside.

As Ned wrapped himself in pastoral duties, I shut myself off in my own lonely, resentful world away from him. My hardworking husband was probably on some level reliving the childhood pain of being shut out by his father, as I became another person in his life to demonstrate the same kind of selfishness. Habits that had protected him from emotional abuse early on in his life maybe caused him to return my disconnectedness with aloofness—who knows?

But one thing was sure: our marriage was always, always, always subservient to whatever my husband considered important in church-related issues, such as church meetings, pastoral counseling sessions, hospital visits, community gatherings, sermon preparations, church communication materials, home visitations to shut-ins, and before long, civil rights issues. I did not feel deserving of any of the full-bore attention he gave to these other causes. Ned was so committed to his new world that he even refused to formally designate one day each week as his day off, as most other pastors did. He wanted the church to know he was always there for them twenty-four seven, no matter how insignificant the issue was. A painful hollowness began to comfortably nest in my psyche.

Unfortunately, I was not the obsessively devoted, uncomplaining cheerleader he was wanting and needing. And on the other side of the coin, he was not the caring, enthusiastic husband I was wanting and needing, either. Great pieces of our beautiful marriage dream seemed to be evaporating.

The months progressed. No teaching job offer had come along, so I tried turning a great deal of energy into decorating our home and taking on sewing projects. However, none of these activities were enough to fill the emptiness that consumed me. I felt trapped. Just getting out of the house on my own was next to impossible. We lived a long way from libraries, commercial places, or even bus lines, and finances dictated we share one car—and that would be the car Ned took each day to work.

Who would have thought, but that notorious car became the cause of a major crack in the veneer of our relationship. Before my marriage, I had worked hard to become a self-sufficient young woman. I felt almost delirious with happiness knowing that I could truly be in charge of my own destiny, and as far as I was concerned, my destiny was going to include a grand car. Purchased after graduation as another step toward self-sufficiency, this car—a

21

classy black two-door Pontiac Tempest with elegant red leather upholstery—brought a great sense of joy to me.

On the other hand, Ned didn't own an automobile when we got married. Therefore, my beautiful automobile became the official family transportation. My car became *our* car. And every day as Ned drove out of the driveway in what had been *my* car, resentment would consume me. Then a sense of shame for my selfish resentment would follow. It was so absolutely fitting that the car be a Tempest!

At breakfast one cool winter morning, I was once again trying to talk about my feelings of homesickness. Thinking back on it, our inability to discuss problems in a healthy way was stunning. We were a poster couple for emotional illiteracy. I felt as though I were confronting a brick wall when I said, "I just don't want you to go away and leave me alone again today." Ned impatiently responded with, "I have to go to work. You know I have hospital visits this morning and the Sunday bulletin to put together this afternoon. My God, Molly, I have a job to do."

As usual, he was the adult with an important agenda while I was the unimportant child. Ned would tolerate this immature behavior only momentarily before his resolute temper would kick in. He abruptly ended the discussion by angrily jumping to his feet and storming out the kitchen door, heading straight for the carport. This was typical for Ned when confronted with my despondence, he would disappear for hours and hours at a time—in our one and only car.

This morning was different, though. I jumped up and followed him out the back door to the carport. I saw him climb into my beautiful black Tempest. He put an exclamation point on his important litany of responsibilities for the day by slamming the door shut.

I got to the carport at the exact moment Ned started the car. Not wanting to be left alone in the house again, I quickly grabbed the car door handle on the passenger side and began to pull the door open as the car started in reverse. With the car suddenly moving backward, my hand slid off the door handle while Ned was pushing his foot down on the gas pedal. Then the passenger-side door—now open—engaged with the sturdy support post at the corner of the carport. In an instant, it happened. The passenger-side door just peeled off of the car at the hinges as smooth as warm butter covering a piece of hot toast. The forlorn door, quite amazingly, dropped gently over into the grass at my feet.

I stood, stunned, looking at the lovely red leather interior of my car door lying dead in the grass in front of me. Then, of all things, our insatiably nosy neighbor, Mrs. Ross, came galloping out of her house next door and over to our driveway demanding to know, "What happened?"

Mrs. Ross was, I'm certain, a top graduate of a highly rated school for snoops, and her abilities to gape, stare, and peer at us all hours of the day and night were noteworthy, indeed. Unfortunately for her, though, her overt neighborly curiosity prevented any further discussion between Ned and me; we may have had our differences, but we always made every effort to keep our verbal disagreements outside the earshot of others. So we both clammed up.

Ned had quickly stopped the car when a large open space where the door had been appeared beside him in the front seat. He climbed out of the car and, with great ceremony, walked solemnly around the back of the vehicle to where the large door lay unmoving in the grass. Neither of us uttered a sound. In my astonishment, though, I watched him move as if in slow motion. With no wasted energy, he bent over and picked up the orphaned door, a look of disdain flooding his face. He slid the detached door sideways through the now-huge opening onto the floor behind the front seat.

Ned's actions were performed with the finesse of a man who, it would appear, was frequently asked to retrieve detached car doors from grassy spaces. Without even a second thought, he seemed to know just what to do to take control of the situation, and with great manliness, he did, each movement completed with the exacting precision of a Prussian general. When he finished the task, he marched back around the car. Still without a word, he slid into the driver's seat, slamming shut the remaining door. With this show of force, the whole car shook strangely, probably owing to the enormous hole in the passenger side of the vehicle. This oddity didn't slow him down a bit, however. Continuing to behave as though nothing had happened, my husband started the car again, rapidly backing down the driveway and driving off down the street.

I can still see clearly in my mind's eye Ned sitting behind the wheel of my magnificent car, pulling out of the driveway and driving off with a gigantic open space in the passenger side of the vehicle, just as though there were nothing amiss. The snapped-off car door appeared as if it were a respected family member propped up sedately behind him in the back seat.

I swallowed hard, trying to process what had just happened. Then I remembered I was still standing there next to my in-your-face neighbor. All of a sudden, it seemed like a scene right out of a Laurel and Hardy movie. Unfortunately, though, Mrs. Ross didn't go away at the end of the scene as I was hoping she would. She remained right there next to me continuing her loud, rude questions: "What happened? What on earth has happened?" All I could think was how stupid the questions were because I thought it was perfectly clear what had happened. She had obviously witnessed the whole incredible scene.

Anyway, it appeared to me that I should be the one asking questions, questions like: "Didn't your mother ever teach you how important it is to mind your own business?" Mrs. Ross surely had missed her mother's pearls of wisdom on that topic.

So I quickly found my way back into the house without uttering a word to my curious neighbor. Luckily, she didn't follow. Back in the house, I dropped down onto a kitchen chair, shaking in amazed disbelief. How could it be that here I was again, trapped in my lonely world? Despite the audacious drama my husband and I had performed for the world to witness, it would appear my spouse was still tone deaf to my loneliness, lacking the interest to try to resolve the situation whatsoever.

How could this be, I asked myself. *How—could—this—be?*

CHAPTER FOUR

Crawdads

Despite my on-and-off struggles with depression, life bubbled along in an interesting new direction that first year. Church involvement filled our social needs as our personal world expanded. With a sense of shared excitement, we took up the challenge of exploring our adopted community whenever Ned could allow himself to unwind for a few hours.

Together we would drive around our neighborhood to find places close by to shop, eat, and buy gas. We were delighted to find a little fast food place, Pork Castle, over on Airport Boulevard, not far from the church where we could get delicious barbecue pork sandwiches, a Mobile specialty. Exploring farther afield, we fell in love with the spectacular white sand beaches on Dauphin Island. One-day jaunts to New Orleans were amazing fun when Ned would allow himself a few hours free time. Mary's Place, a tiny seafood restaurant swallowed up in an old wreck of a house, was tucked into swampy undergrowth in the middle of nowhere in the southern end of Mobile County. Serving incredible gumbo, this jewel was one of our favorite new destinations when Ned would spare the time.

Just seven years old, Holy Cross Lutheran Church, Ned's new parish, was housed in a beautiful, well-appointed complex. Long, picturesque windows lining the sanctuary walls looked out on beautiful costal landscaping. The buildings, tastefully set back from a major highway threading through the Mobile suburbs, were surrounded by tall graceful pines and lush, semitropical plantings all situated on a huge lot. It was a perfect gathering place for a socially promising Christian congregation in Mobile. As a respite to my loneliness, I discovered welcome satisfaction in church activities in this center of congregational life. From the start, I was eager to try my wings as pastor's wife. I found pleasure in Sunday-morning services and in the many congregation events occurring in the church building on Airport Boulevard.

Holy Cross parishioners were an assorted collection of white, middle-class, mostly educated folk, who owned their own businesses or were in management positions of some kind or another. Few women parishioners were employed outside the home. One memorable exception was a college professor, Dr. Helen Lindsey. Most families owned their own comfortable houses in nearby communities, and many had young children.

These folks were energetically devoted to the Holy Cross community as the center of their social lives. Interestingly, about one-third of the members were not originally from the South but were from other parts of the country. They had arrived in beautiful Mobile Bay world as a result of job transfers—usually in the paper-mill industry. It was interesting watching these transplants take on the mantle of traditional white Southern cultural values with eagerness. They appeared to want to feel like they really belonged. I understood that feeling completely.

Sunday morning was the highlight of my week. I took great care in getting my appearance just right. Comments and rumors from some in the congregation had gotten back to me very early on regarding my appearance—comments like: "She has a fashion sense that really doesn't fit here in Mobile" and "I wouldn't describe her as real skinny." (Nor would I, as it happened.) So I always knew that what I wore and how I looked would probably be scrutinized in detail.

Ned encouraged me at the end of each worship service to stand at the church door with him as parishioners walked out. This helped me feel like I was a part of his church life, even if only to a small degree. The big plus to this was that greeting people as they left helped me get to know members more quickly.

The role of pastor's wife meant that I needed to do some serious planning as to what I would wear at church events. For Sunday mornings, I usually chose things that were probably considered a bit out of the cultural mold for Mobile, like a great cranberry-colored two-piece Italian knit suit. The three-quarter sleeve, longish jacket buttoned up the front to a Nehru-type collar while the pencil-thin skirt ended just above the knee. The outfit, paired with color-coordinated heels, white gloves, and a cranberry pillbox hat, got a rather judgmental reaction from the congregation—too high fashion, they called it. I suppose the look was more common in bigger metropolitan areas than Mobile, but I liked the confidence it gave me.

Sunday-morning church attendance began to increase, and Ned was developing a group of folks who strongly supported him and especially loved his sermons. He had the luxury of following a pastor who had defined religious life very narrowly. In fact, the former pastor's dismal view of what it meant to be a Christian had left many congregation members longing for a more tolerant and less judgmental pastor, and they cheerfully found that in liberal-leaning Ned Milner.

As the church began to grow, Ned threw himself into all kinds of ministerial tasks. One family in the congregation had newborn twins, both of whom were critically ill for the first few months of their lives. Ned spent long hours—day and night—in the hospital with the family as the weeks went by. The experience of trying to be there for this family brought him to ultimately became a volunteer hospital chaplain. And surprisingly, his non-Lutheran, unorthodox, and radical view on communion—that it was open to anyone who wanted to partake of it—at first took folks back a bit, but then it was wholly embraced with resounding enthusiasm. He saw himself as moving the congregation into what he considered the enlightenment of the 1960s. And, at first, this youngish collection of congregants was happy to go along.

Church life was good for the first several months. And, for a while, so as not to rock the boat, Ned actively did very little to move the highly charged racial agenda. He quite liked the idea of being the beloved pastor of a young, thriving church. And I, too, liked—better yet, *loved*—the idea! This piece of my shiny dream seemed alive and well. My role as pastor's wife brought an undeniable sense of satisfaction to me, balancing the otherwise less-than-happy stuff in my life.

A wonderful memory of this time was the first big congregational event after we arrived—a crawdad dinner. Now, I had never even heard of crawdads before, so I could hardly wait to see what all the hoopla was about. Walking into the parish hall the night of the crawdad affair, I was struck with the overwhelming odor of fishiness. On the restaurant-size stove in the church kitchen, huge pots of freshly harvested crawdads—first cousins to small shrimp, in my estimation—were boiling away. Church members were scurrying around with hands ensconced in oven mitts, hauling big pots of the creatures to the sink to drain off the water. Then the funny-looking little pink sea creatures—the crawdads—left in the pots were unceremoniously dumped into big piles on long tables that had been covered with layers of clean butcher paper.

Steaming pots of seafood, easygoing laughter, and conviviality conspired to create a great atmosphere. The evening turned into raucously good fun as we sat around together at the paper-covered tables, hand-shucking tiny crawdads, and swiftly consuming each small pile of carcasses on the spot.

Neither Ned nor I had ever eaten a crawdad before, but both of us loved seafood. We also liked the friendly kidding and joking: "Hey, Yankees! Can your Northern innards take on some true Southern delicacies?" The best part for me was to experience welcoming inclusion by these new friends. The whole scene was loving church community life at its best. It felt good having people show us they liked us. Ned and I were delighted. Quite magically, warmth and good humor broke down cultural barriers. This was, it seemed to me, what the life of a pastor's wife should be like. It pleased me to think I might be fitting into the congregation's expectations.

Unfortunately, though, there was a secret road bump in this happy church picture. The small problem was that I had never fully embraced Lutheran doctrine to the point of actually joining the Lutheran church. Now, that may seem to some like small potatoes, but to loyal, hard-working congregation members, my standoffishness could present a real trust issue for Ned. It meant that the pastor's wife had not signed on, so to speak, as a formal member of his own flourishing congregation, which could be a bit embarrassing for my husband. Ned knew I struggled with some Lutheran concepts, such as infant baptism and the Eucharist, but he always showed great understanding in talking all this theology through with me. While I was well on my way to embracing these faith precepts, I just wasn't quite ready yet to commit to being a full-fledged, official member. It would seem it was the only card I held in my marriage that might possibly have any power over my husband, and I stubbornly held on to it for a very long time.

Thinking back on this conduct, I can see that refusing church membership surely was an act of independence with strong ties, I'm sure, to the feminist movement. However important my lack of membership was to Ned, in my memory, the awkward predicament was never publicly discussed in any church setting. I never attended any other church or participated in different church activities other than at Holy Cross, so there was no overt indication to anyone that I wasn't 100 percent in Ned's corner. But in my heart, I held out on the technicality of church membership, independent little soul that I was, experiencing it as a rather cherished slice of pride, deep inside. And as time went by with other factors and forces impacting my life in wildly unanticipated ways, I never did officially join Holy Cross Lutheran Church—ever.

CHAPTER FIVE

Cocoon Cracks

Just before Christmas, Ned and I were invited to a posh evening holiday party at the home of civil rights activist, Hal Reed. Hal owned a historic antebellum home in Fairhope. The elegant mansion was perched on a huge parcel of land fronting on beautiful Mobile Bay. Driving down the long rambling entry road, we found a line of sturdy poles stuck in the ground every several yards with torches burning brightly at the top. I felt as though a time machine had taken us back a hundred years. Wildly flickering shadows made it appear as though Tara itself might be at the end of the drive. And then the home's shape materialized. Just as the romantic in me had hoped, I saw the grand old home—meticulously restored. We parked and walked up to the ostentatious entrance of the home lined with stately pillars. My heart was full of expectations for the evening as I was certainly not accustomed to attending parties in such classy surroundings.

The interior of the house matched the exterior in authentic restoration. Pricey antique furnishings abounded. Period Christmas decorations with backdrops of bay leaves, pine, and holly extensively filled corners and niches everywhere. A huge

Christmas tree sat in the center of the largest room, spectacular with old-fashioned tree ornaments and small, glowing candles. If Disney had been hired to simulate a prosperous Southern home of 1850 for the evening, it could not have looked any more believable—except for the fact that there was a rich racial mix of serving persons. Pine fragrance filled the rooms, and soft flickering candles everywhere created magical visions. There seemed to be no probable need for electricity in the house that night. Candlelight carried the show.

Guests were mostly civil rights activists whom we had met over the past few months from throughout the Mobile and Baldwin County areas. The venue stood in sharp contrast to other activists' homes we'd visited. I don't remember, if I ever knew, what Hal did for a living. But whatever it was left him quite successful financially. The party was a rare treat in our civil-rights-activist world, to be sure.

The evening gave me a wonderful chance to socialize without my pastor's-wife filter. So far, my social life had been within the confines of church-prescribed experiences. In these gatherings, it was almost like living in a very small town. I was always considering what might be the possible unintended consequences of my words and actions. So I was continually on guard. But at this party, it was unusually nice to be able to do or say whatever, and not have to worry. It seemed a true breath of fresh air.

On this night, I met John Hill, a young casework supervisor for the Mobile County welfare department. During our conversation, I happened to mention my interest in finding some meaningful employment. John told me he thought I might do well as a caseworker for the department, adding there were many vacancies right then. He detailed how I would need to take a civil service exam to qualify, and if successful, I would be placed on a civil service list. The whole idea of potentially becoming a social worker came from out of the blue, but the idea really interested me.

Talking on the way home about John's job suggestion, Ned thought I should look into it since the absence of a teaching offer had left me feeling adrift. Ned had never been against the notion of having a working wife. He just wanted a wife who didn't demand him to redirect any of his time and energy from his compelling commitments to church and civil rights issues. So without much thought, I decided to follow up on the prospect.

Another potential caseworker applicant and I drove to Montgomery a few weeks later to take the civil service exam. As we arrived at the Alabama state capitol building, solemn rows of gray stone steps leading up to the entrance caught my eye. I was impressed but naively did not connect the landmark visual with Governor George Wallace's infamous racist rant, "segregation now, segregation tomorrow, segregation forever," which had been delivered from those very steps just a short time before.

I was pathetically out of touch with so much historical information pertaining to racial issues in my new Southern life. My memory bank did not contain snapshots of such time-noted political scenes as Wallace's nationally prominent comments because I had not been raised to connect to such events. Growing up, I remember asking my mother about the possibility of changes in our lives during the late 1950s because of overt signs of racial unrest in popular magazines. Her counsel to me was to ignore all this kind of upsetting "stuff" because everything was going to stay just as it was. Her words were a smug reassurance that nothing was going to change in our pitty-pat white privileged world. Fed this kind of advice, it was no surprise, then, that racial unrest was, for me, a topic to be simply ignored.

The official family narrative had left me in a comfortable cocoon of blatant ignorance. My fundamentalist Christian heritage had wrapped this cocoon in the singular view that life should be about making sure you are saved. Nothing else mattered—except for the unspoken, insidious, but very real goal of succeeding in a capitalist system. And as a female, this goal clearly translated into marrying well—meaning marrying a man who would financially provide a life of good things for me. My own aspirations should be sublimated as I followed the family mantra—get saved and marry well. Something extraordinary was happening in my new marriage, however. I was beginning to feel a strong need to break out of that thick, suffocating casing of the family cocoon. Living with the likes of social activist Ned Milner, I was being forced to face up to the fact that I had a great deal of soul-searching to do.

It wasn't long before a letter came from the state of Alabama saying I had passed the civil service exam, and soon I was offered a job in the Mobile County welfare department. Accepting the job offer required I attend a two-week training session for new hires. A veteran caseworker, Bella Fowler, conducted the caseworker training, which provided me with valuable insights into a system I knew little about. She was especially intent in making sure we had a strong sense of empathy for our welfare clients. I have never forgotten her wise words regarding the notion of expectations. She told us everyone is given a finite amount of psychic energy each day. When that is gone—it is gone. If that energy has been expended on trying to figure out how to have water turned back on in the house, or where to find money to buy food for the next meal, it doesn't matter. When that energy is gone—marginal energy is left for other goals, so expectations need to fit specific circumstances, not the other way around. Bella's sound advice served me well in the weeks and months to come.

I was excited about the caseworker career. My experience as a housewife had left me uninspired and depressed. The feminist movement had made strong inroads over the past few years, shattering stereotypical norms about how women could live, and I had privately bought into those concepts. In contrast, long-held cultural beliefs, especially in the South, held tightly to the notion that a woman's role should be solely that of a housewife and mother. This idea was especially valued within religious settings. Most folks believed that a woman who made any other choices in life contributed to a hazardous breakdown of society. Without a doubt, as a minister's wife, I tapped into this sentiment on some level. At the same time, though, I was plagued by a longing for something else in my life. The resulting guilt left me unsettled and really rather unpleasant to be around. But when I sat down and considered all that was at stake, I ultimately didn't seem to have any choice but to follow my heart. And my heart said—get out of the house and do something that makes you feel better about yourself. So I did.

And in taking that step, I began to find an extraordinary sense of satisfaction. Buying a second car was one of the first tasks for us when I was hired in my job. We settled on a bouncy little blue Opel.

Like slow drops of water at first, my worldview began to expand when I was driving about in my new car each day conducting the business of welfare work. I seemed to find that proximity with poverty in both black and white communities gifted me with unanticipated spiritual growth. These experiences tore at the casing of my family cocoon. I couldn't help but see stunning examples of how issues of equality were perverted because of intolerance. Unexpectedly, my life was being transformed by the witness to intimate feelings of hopelessness and despair.

CHAPTER SIX

It Gunna Be
All Right

As the sun started its daily trek across the morning sky, I was already uncomfortable in the increasing temperature. In fact, in Mobile's coastal, junglelike climate, the humidity was so thick you could rinse your carport down and mildew would appear before the structure even dried. So I was on the road by seven a.m., even though I was definitely not an early-morning person. My primary goal was to finish field visits to welfare clients' homes before the fierce heat of midday. Adding to the heat was the noxious odor of sulfur dioxide, which usually did a number on my psyche, sometimes even leaving me a little disoriented and nauseous.

Saraland and Satsuma, rural communities just a few miles north of Mobile, were my destinations. I was responsible for welfare clients in those small neighborhoods. For the past few months, it had been my job to visit the home of every family on my assigned list at least once every few weeks. The rural roads, mostly free of people or cars, made the job of finding client houses a huge challenge. Signs and address markers were almost nonexistent.

The first client on my list was Addie Mae. Her shotgun house sat in a forlorn cluster of similar places just outside the tiny crossroads of Saraland on a treeless red-dirt patch of ground. The term "shotgun" refers to the simple architectural design of a narrow one-story house with a combined kitchen/living room across the front and a long, straight hall running through the house from the front room to the back door. Off the hall on either side are small rooms used for bedrooms. The design—very utilitarian in concept—is certainly lacking anything aesthetic. These default houses, common through rural black communities in the South, are usually poorly constructed. They are often perched on mini stilts, probably to discourage snakes and other undesirable creatures from entering. Addie Mae's house and the other dwellings close by sat lonely amid rather desolate surroundings.

I slowly edged my car haphazardly onto the rust-colored dirt in front of Addie Mae's house, then turned off the engine. Trying to get myself pulled together, I took out a tissue and patted the perspiration from my damp face. Then, gathering up my client file, I straightened my cotton shift dress around me. I'd intentionally chosen to wear the home-sewn dress to appear as plain Jane as possible. I believed that my welfare clients had enough to contend with already. Adding the emotional baggage of a caseworker marching into a house, unannounced, dressed in clothes economically unattainable for them seemed like it would only contribute to the high-handedness of the situation. So I was grateful for the sewing skills my mother and grandmother had taught me. I also thought that wearing my own homemade dresses might help keep me more grounded, as I was rather unsure of myself in the new job.

I tried to put myself in each client's place. Really, I didn't see this welfare-worker-visitation stuff as much more than, at best, a patronizing activity. I worked at trying to create a nonthreatening atmosphere during home visits, but I was not sure my Pollyanna efforts made any difference whatsoever. Daily, I saw the look of long-standing distrust in my clients' eyes. And it was because of my naive efforts at trying to build trust that I ended up in such an emotional mess that day.

Familiar with Addie Mae's file, I reviewed her basic information again: twentysomething client, seasonal agricultural worker, and mother of four young children. She had no employable skills, no formal education, no family resources, and little community support. To think she really could improve her situation was improbable. She'd had the misfortune of being born into a family and a community of poverty where the only expectation people had for her was to do the best she could each day, desperately struggling with what little she had been given. The pathetically inadequate amount of welfare subsistence when a client had no income did nothing to instill any sense of hope for better things to come. Her life had been forged by cruel and unforgiving forces. She was one of many women I worked with who found themselves in similar circumstances. Black skin and poverty had combined to deal Addie Mae and others like her an incredibly unjust hand.

Out of the car windshield, I gazed at the scene in front of me. Overhead, the sky was a brilliant, shimmering blue. The sun was so bright that shadows seemed etched into the ground. I somehow found the structures, humans, and animals almost indefinable. It was as if the sun had produced a huge, surreal paintbrush. The brush, dripping with watercolor paint, had splashed faded sepia-toned sadness over everything and everyone. My mind almost reeled at the scene. For a moment, I was unsettled. It appeared as if I had unexplainably ended up in an alien place. I had nothing in my memory bank that connected to anything in the scene before me.

I asked myself how I had ended up here. But then the practical voice took over; I threw out the weird notion of an alien place, pulled myself up, and determined to get about doing what I believed I had been hired to do.

In an uncomplicated way, I saw myself as a fragile lifeline for the welfare clients assigned to me. It didn't take long to feel that a great deal of what I was asked to do as a caseworker was patronizing.

And that part of the job made me feel incredibly uncomfortable. The lives I encountered each day were emotionally and financially forsaken. Hope seemed nonexistent to most. So my job, patronizing or not, kept the welfare subsistence pipeline open to them when there was usually nothing else. Right or wrong, my sense of pragmatism kept me trudging on.

In front of the house, I saw a handful of small children playing among a spattering of resilient chickens and an unbelievably thin dog. But sadly, I saw no toys, only sticks, scraps of cardboard, and the odd mail flyer. A decrepit empty wooden box sat close to the house and seemed to be the center of interest. The children's clothing was ragged and threadbare. But then I heard the engaging sound of children's laughter. The happy noise belied everything I saw. And the cheerful sound pulled me out of my funk a little, and I got out of the car.

But as I walked closer to Addie Mae's house, I found my heart beginning to sink into a rather deep morass. There was nothing in my field of vision that gave off any sense of comfort or ease—everything was sepia toned—stark, worn out, and austere. I knew each step brought me closer to hearing another chapter in a welfare client's narrative, which never seemed to have a happy ending. The air felt immense with hopelessness. As it usually happened when I reached this point in a home visit, I began to feel a shortness of breath. Getting air into my lungs became more and more difficult. Perspiration trickled down the back of my neck and onto my dress.

Climbing the few steps to the rickety front porch brought me face-to-face with an amazingly thin woman sitting on an ancient kitchen chair. Addie Mae's elderly auntie Dourt sat with a profoundly hollow look about her. Her beautiful coffee-with-cream-colored thin boney hands rested elegantly in her lap. She had a stately aura, almost like that of a royal queen. Her eyes were not connecting with mine, but instead she stared straight ahead, motionless. Dressed in the remnants of a simple cotton button-up housedress, her hair was tightly tied in a faded blue kerchief in a tight knot on top. On her feet were appalling things that must have been cheap slide-on shoes sometime back, but after extreme wear, they now just barely hung on her. The thin flaps provided little protection for her heavily calloused feet.

I smiled and said hello, then waited for her to respond. The words, slow and deliberate, came from deep inside the desolate woman. She told me in a soft voice with a melodic rural Southern drawl that Addie Mae had been "feeling poorly." It was as though any focused energy Auntie Dourt might have once possessed had long since drained from her. She seemed to be simply a shell existing only in the sadness of the moment.

Auntie Dourt's spattering of words, thrown slowly out into the breeze, told me that her niece, Addie Mae, had been sick for several days. She added that her niece had been without medical assistance, or even medicine, during that time. Auntie Dourt slowly pulled her boney frame upright and started taking small steps toward the door. She opened the dilapidated wood screen, and I walked in to go and see Addie Mae for myself. Each step I took increased the feeling of dread I had about what was to come next.

I followed Auntie Dourt through the sparse living space and down the hallway to one of the small rooms. The space gave off the very intimate feeling of accommodating sleeping needs for several people. I walked into the room and saw that the walls were covered with layers and layers of old newspapers, probably a practical effort at insulation. Ammonia fumes from a cleaning mixture filled my nostrils. There were only two clumsy-looking iron bed frames in the room with little more than piles of rags for mattresses.

In one of the beds, I found Addie Mae's long, thin frame clothed in a threadbare housedress. She lay curled in a nest of tatty bedclothes with her bare legs and feet pulled up to her midsection. The defined muscles in her young mahogany-colored face were tense with pain. A scraggly kerchief tied tightly in a knot on top of her head completely covered her hair. Her large dark eyes opened slowly. Soft moaning came floating up from her throat. Then, in just a few almost unintelligible words, she told me she had pain in her midsection where her hands were clutching her stomach. Addie Mae was less than articulate about her complaint, but it was obvious that she needed help beyond what I could give her.

The tiny space felt almost devoid of oxygen. I was overcome with a feeling of helplessness. I tried to breathe deeply and thought to myself: What on earth was I doing there? This was not what I thought I had signed on for as a caseworker. But then, if the truth be known, I really hadn't known what I'd signed on for. I had only gone down this caseworker road as a stand-in for what I really wanted to do. I wanted to be a teacher. I had spent two years of my life happily teaching middle school kids, and that was where my heart was. How had things gotten so mixed up?

Standing in Addie Mae's bedroom, I realized that my rather blasé decision to become a caseworker—after any prospects of teaching had slipped away—had landed me in some heavy-duty emotional hot water. I was not at all prepared for this situation. Looking back, my naiveté seems extraordinary to me.

Each day in this new career, I witnessed unbelievably misfortunate things happening to people. And in each case, I had the sad feeling I could do little to really change the situation. Just the week before, I worked with a large family trying to care for a particularly sick baby. The water had been shut off in their home because their welfare assistance money had been used to pay for medicine. It was not uncommon for less-than-sufficient welfare assistance to cause disastrous outcomes. Often, a client would have to choose between paying the rent or the utility bill—as a small amount toward each one would not do the job. I desperately wanted to change each and every client's situation as the unhappy stories piled on, but the truth was I was not able to make much of a difference in anyone's life.

While my job was giving me an unexpected firsthand education on how people tried to survive the onslaught of poverty, it was also forcing me to reexamine my own values. I quickly began to see in sharp detail the unloving view of life I'd had growing up. The simplistic notion that most people got just about what they deserved in life was rooted deep in my psyche. This insidious concept was coupled with the idea that if you just worked hard enough, you could achieve anything you might want. And the most disingenuous myth of all seemed to be that poverty was likely the punishment for lazy and/or bad behavior.

Forced to consider these beliefs one by one, I discovered that I had been living in a world of insensitivity. The irony was that I had always thought I was a person who showed a generosity of spirit. I thought, after all, I was a Christian woman, and had been ever since my public religious conversion at the age of ten when I'd given witness to my faith by walking down the aisle of my Baptist church. The stark truth, upon deeper examination, showed I was completely mistaken on this score, though. I looked inside and saw that callousness took up all the space where tolerance and kindness should be living. So beginning to let go of this closely held family belief system became important to me.

And then what did I really know about good practices in the field of social work anyway? The honest answer would be little at best! Yet there I was on a beautiful day in Saraland, Alabama, staring into the face of complete desperation. A voice inside reminded me—there but for the grace of God go I. Mysteriously, I felt compelled to try to turn the unjust economic system around to help Addie Mae. Unfortunately, though, there was no "caseworkers' manual" I could pull out and refer to for a hands-on solution to this particular problem. Nor was there a booklet of policies and procedures detailing a workable resolution. I was at a loss to know what to do. But it was clear that I had to do something, and do it quickly.

It was just three short tumultuous years after the Freedom Summer project of 1964—a nonviolent effort by civil rights activists to integrate Mississippi's segregated political system. Residents and volunteers were met by extraordinary violence from the Ku Klux Klan, including murders, bombings, kidnappings, and torture. And the Mississippi state line was less than thirty miles west of where I was standing in the rural crossroads known as Saraland,

Alabama. I was aware the civil rights movement had a long way to go to even begin to right the unending list of injustices. Yet this problem with Addie Mae stemming from poverty and racism was right there in front of me. It demanded I do something immediately. Patience was not an option.

Collecting my thoughts, I decided to drive Addie Mae to the nearest hospital emergency room. It was obvious her support system had no means of transportation, and I had a working vehicle. The plan was clear. Auntie Dourt would stay with the children, and I would get Addie Mae carefully tucked into my car and drive her off to the closest hospital.

I found myself with Addie Mae seated beside me as I came upon the hospital I had seen several times before just outside of Saraland. It turned out to be a rather new large community building officially calling itself an infirmary, and this was just what I believed was needed.

Parking close to the entrance, I helped Addie Mae out and maneuvered her into the building toward the area marked "Emergency." Then, without asking anyone, because we couldn't find any staff, I helped Addie Mae onto an empty gurney. Almost immediately, I felt uncomfortable—almost like we were there but we weren't really there; I don't know how else to describe it. Trying to put this weird feeling aside, I took a seat near her. I felt self-satisfied, believing we had arrived at a place where Addie Mae could begin to get some help. I had done what my moral compass had directed me to do.

Then the crazy stuff began. Addie Mae lay motionless on the gurney, curled up on her side and covered with a clean white sheet. Her eyes appeared diverted off into the distance, focusing on nothing in particular. In retrospect, I know I should have noticed the haunting look of fear on her face, but I didn't. The emergency room doctor and nurse—both white—walked past Addie Mae and me as if we didn't exist. At first, their elusive behavior didn't register in my head. I believed they were busy with other patients and we just had to wait our turn. But then the doctor and nurse continued to walk around us, deliberately refusing to provide any help to Addie Mae, or even to acknowledge that she existed.

After about a half hour, a light bulb finally went off in my brain. I began to understand what was actually going on—silly, naive me. We were, of course, experiencing unabashed racism. The simple truth of the matter was that Addie Mae was being ignored because of her skin color. I'd missed the signs outside the building, if there were any, specifying what color of skin was required for entrance. How could I have been so culturally ignorant? From kindergarten through high school, I had attended completely integrated schools. I had sat in classrooms, played on playgrounds, and nurtured friendships with black children throughout my school years. Obviously, my racial worldview did not fit this situation.

When the notion of bigotry finally found space in my psyche, I became unglued. Popping to my feet in a sudden rush of fury, I was filled with indignation. My heart was beating wildly. My cheeks were raging hot, and I pulled together my best *how dare you!* spirit. In a loud, angry voice, I asked the attending nurse, "Why is nothing being done for this woman? She's been lying in pain on this gurney being ignored for too long."

With an iciness that froze everyone within earshot, the nurse in charge answered loudly in a voice slathered with Southern molasses, "There isn't a thing we can do for her, honey. You might just as well take her back home." The nurse followed with another frosty barb: "Or you could go to the Negro clinic down in Mobile if you want to."

I was stunned! The thought that these medical professionals were supposed to take responsibility for this woman in pain seemed to be a foreign concept. And aside from my unsuccessful rather dramatic performance, I was clueless as to how to force any compliance. Even as Addie Mae lay there unmoving, she was much more savvy about the unspoken truths of the situation than I was. I finally realized that her whole demeanor radiated fear. Struggling with what were clearly overwhelming feelings of humiliation, she ultimately convinced me in quiet, halting words, salted with tears: "I jus' wanna go on back."

Unbelievably frustrated, I found that all I could do was to help Addie Mae up off the gurney and slowly walk with her back to the car. It felt as though I was in the middle of a horrible nightmare. I was shaking with anger as we were met with scathing looks from the white faces in the waiting room. I had been blind to this visible hatred when we'd first come in, but on our way out, I was astounded by the awful energy we encountered.

Just as we reached the parking lot, Addie Mae and I stopped and looked up at the same moment, as though some force had silently jolted our attention away from the car. We both immediately looked to the side of the building. There, in a shaded doorway area, we saw a figure of a person who must have been the janitor. The short middle-aged black man dressed in simple, well-worn denim coveralls and a worn T-shirt stood alone with a broom grasped tightly in his hand. He stared at us with a look of extraordinary sadness on his face. As our eyes met his, we drew unexpected strength from his faithful witness to this humiliating drama. It was but another scene in the centuries-long, mostly unrecorded story of cruel racism. After a few moments, Addie Mae and I climbed into the car and drove off. The memory of that sunny morning in Saraland, Alabama, stands out as a truly surreal experience that haunts my daydreams, even decades later.

My plan to provide assistance to my client had hit the brick wall known as bigotry. I was at the end of my rope as far as my options were concerned. I didn't know where the Negro clinic was in Mobile. Besides, I knew the place wasn't even open every day. So I decided against attempting the forty-mile round-trip drive. Instead, I scaled down my plan, and wallowing in suffocating sadness, I stopped at a tiny, shoddy storefront building that advertised groceries along the dirt road back to Addie Mae's house. With a ridiculously fragile sense of hope, I went in to see if there was an over-the-counter product I could purchase to help Addie Mae. Out of desperation, I bought some silly, self-help wonder cure that pompously promised healing for most all afflictions. As I handed it over to Addie Mae with some basic directions on how often to take the stuff, a ridiculous feeling of promise for maybe a small bit of help for my friend welled up inside me. In the stark light of day, it seemed like an unbelievably foolish promise was all I had left to offer.

In utter defeat, I returned Addie Mae to her home. Helping her back into that small bedroom, I was filled all of a sudden with fear as I contemplated the thought that she might possibly die from her malady. What would happen to her children and Auntie Dourt? How would I be able to live with that outcome? My hands grew cold at the thought.

The lack of options to help her left me anguished as she rearranged herself back in the same position as when I'd first found her a few hours before. I stood there over the bed for a few moments, then I slowly took her hand in mine. My eyes filled with tears as I tried to tell her how deeply sorry I was for what had just happened. Her eyes met mine, and somehow—surprisingly—she seemed to convey to me in a few words that I shouldn't worry. Her soft voice, filled with extraordinary dignity, reached out to me, "It gunna be all right."

I left the room and slowly walked back to my car. I opened the door and dropped onto the seat behind the steering wheel. This had been my first official opportunity to come face-to-face with a situation where "correct" skin color trumped all other considerations. I sat for a few moments, trying to compose my thoughts and figure out what had just happened. My hands shook, and tears of frustration ran down my cheeks. I had never felt so completely helpless—so miserable—ever before in my entire life.

My mind became paralyzed with shame. I began the haunting process of questioning whether I should have done more to help Addie Mae. Perhaps some strong threats in the emergency room would have made a bit of difference. But the truth of the matter was that I really didn't have any idea what I could have used as a serious threat. I grappled with the fact that all my self-righteous drama in the emergency room hadn't made an ounce of difference. In fact, my behavior probably had made things worse for her. After all, she had to continue to live in the community, not me.

Then my brain jumped to my underlying reason for being there in the first place: to check the family's living circumstances in order to validate ongoing need for county assistance. A supervisor might say I was not there to be an EMT and use my car as a medical emergency vehicle. I could hear the voice of the caseworker job trainer, Bella, in my head telling me that if I believed Addie Mae's physical needs were mine to attend to, I should have managed the situation in a more hands-off, dispassionate way. I should have helped Addie Mae and Auntie Dourt come up with their own solution to the problem—a little like finding yourself standing next to someone whose hair has caught on fire and, instead of attempting to immediately put out the fire yourself, you run around with everyone involved looking for a possible fire extinguisher.

So I had to finally accept the fact that the incredibly frustrating situation was not going to be resolved that day. In humiliation, I turned on the car ignition and drove slowly away. The next day, and for several days after, I made unscheduled visits to Addie Mae's house. Over time, I found her beginning to feel a bit better, and for that I was deeply grateful.

But the episode had left me intensely shaken, and deeply frustrated. My wretched feelings had unknowingly etched through skin and bone and into my very soul. What I didn't understand about the experience, but would come to grips with later, was that my tears in the car were baptizing me into a stunning new realty— life in Jim Crow Land. And the grace I was privileged to encounter in Addie Mae would be a source of enormous strength, sustaining me through the incredible weeks and months ahead.

CHAPTER SEVEN

Gee's Bend

Ned found great satisfaction in the work of energizing his young church. At first, he preached somewhat cautious sermons, trying to establish himself as a middle-of-the-road guy. He didn't want to antagonize the congregation with a heavy dose of racial-equality rhetoric right at the start. But as our lives were transformed by unexpected events, Ned's focus changed quickly. Issues of race and justice soon became his obsession, both in the pulpit and out of the pulpit. Our trip to Gee's Bend, Alabama, was primary in moving this agenda.

Arnie Voigt told us about a workshop to be held in a place with an odd-sounding name. Arnie and his wife, Judy, had been our closest friends since we'd arrived in Mobile. Arnie was the pastor at Faith Lutheran Church, a well-established, historic black congregation in Mobile. Both Ned's church, Holy Cross, and Arnie's church, Faith, were part of the same national Lutheran church body. Both churches were first assignments for each young pastor. But Arnie's challenge was a little different from Ned's in that Arnie was a white man assigned to pastor an all-black congregation. Arnie had an eager openness to connect with the black experience as much as he could. As a response to this goal, he encouraged his wife, Judy, along with Ned and me, to attend the Gee's Bend workshop with him. The event was being promoted as a consciousness-raising weekend to help participants gain a better understanding of life in rural black Alabama. Since all four of us had grown up and, except for Ned, been educated in the North, the chance to learn more about life in the rural South, especially a black community, seemed like a good plan—even though we had no idea what to expect.

The Gee's Bend workshop was being organized by the Selma Inter-religious Project, or SIP, a coalition of ten religious denominations who had joined forces in supporting civil rights causes in the aftermath of the violent 1965 Selma March. Often referred to as the Black Belt, we learned that much of central Alabama, where Gee's Bend is located, was rural and almost unreachable. The director of SIP, a young Episcopal priest, Father Francis X. Walter, had organized the event to be hosted by the residents of the Gee's Bend community. Arnie was on the SIP contact list, so when he came up with the Gee's Bend workshop idea, it didn't take much coaxing on his part to get us all to agree to go.

None of us knew anything about Gee's Bend, located in Alberta, directly south of Selma—except Arnie, who knew that Martin Luther King Jr. had visited there two years earlier. The city's geography had served to keep its black residents significantly isolated. Situated on land located in a large bend of the Alabama River, with no bridge crossing the expansive waterway at any point, there was only one semi-reliable way in and out of the community: a miles-long, poorly maintained county road.

On a Friday afternoon in January 1967, the four of us left Mobile to drive 140 miles north to our workshop. About two hours later, we turned off the main highway in Alberta where a broken-down sign with a crusty arrow pointed the way to Gee's Bend. The stretch of pavement we turned onto—hardly a road at all—was gently winding, and miles and miles long. There were no dwellings, commercial buildings, or structures of any kind along the road after the Alberta turnoff. Continuing past scrub oak, scattered pine, and a good deal of thick, messy undergrowth, the terrain was flat. As the light faded, none of us knew what lay at the southern end of this wannabe highway, except the name of the place: Gee's Bend.

Finally, the road dead-ended into a flat clearing about half a mile wide. Several small ramshackle dwellings sat in forlorn groupings. Constructed mostly of little more than tar paper and random lengths of well-worn boards, the structures appeared to be homes. Two or three larger buildings sat on a maze of squiggly dirt tracks among rambling, expansive oaks and towering pine trees. Gee's Bend was certainly rural and completely isolated from the outside world. It was so secluded that I felt almost as though we had disappeared into another universe.

A few cars were parked close to what appeared to be a church-like structure with lights glowing warmly inside. Pulling up next to it, we climbed out of the car and stretched our legs. It was almost six o'clock, and darkness was rolling into niches and corners everywhere. Surprisingly cold air easily penetrated my light clothing, and the majestic pine trees shared a heavy dose of earthy fragrance.

Then Father Francis Walter came out of the church to officially welcome us. Francis, a dark-haired young man dressed in casual slacks and clerical shirt with white collar, pulled a thick button-up sweater around his shoulders and readjusted his large, dark-rimmed glasses. He chuckled engagingly. Then, with a spark of humor in his eyes, Father Walter decidedly announced, "You all gunna have a fantastic time in Gee's Bend!" The workshop would be our introduction to Francis Walter, a remarkably courageous, below-the-radar hero in the civil rights world in Alabama.

The old floorboards creaked loudly as we walked up the steps of the wood-frame church. Inside the rickety double doors, the large open room had a small platform at the far end holding a pulpit and a few chairs. The ceiling height gave a sense of dignity to the space, and it accommodated a few generic hanging lights that could have come from an old school building. Assorted long, narrow windows lined each wall. Neat rows of rough-cut church pews facing the platform filled the middle section of the space. Situated in the back center of the room, a large potbellied iron stove glowed brightly. I sensed the whole room had been strategically planned around that robust centerpiece—as if the presence of the Almighty herself flowed from the fiery energy inside. The welcome warmth the fire gave off rolled over me in soft waves, combining with the pungent odor of burning wood.

The back of the church was filled with a collection of tables surrounded by decrepit wooden folding chairs. Generous bowls of fried food, collard greens, macaroni salad, and sweet potato pie were spread out over the first table in the row. As the warmth from the fire surrounded me, enticing food odors crept into my consciousness, seductively drawing me farther into the room.

Of the twenty-five or so people there, four or five others looked much like we did—white folks in casual middle-class attire. The remainder were residents of the Gee's Bend community. Each resident was dressed in extremely well-worn, clean clothes—the men mostly in long-sleeved work shirts and pants, or threadbare bib-front overalls, and the women in simple, homemade cotton dresses covered with well-worn sweaters. The faces of the Gee's Bend residents magnified lives of struggle.

As I was introduced to our Gee's Bend hosts, I became familiar with surnames like "Witherspoon," "Williams," and "Pettway." Our conversation quickly turned to food, and one of our hosts, Mrs. Witherspoon, quieted all of us. She gathered her hands together in the stillness and raised her arms, pronouncing a heartfelt blessing on the generous meal. Her speech was immersed in a rich, rural Southern drawl that made me have to slowly sort out the words in my brain to make sense of the prayer. "Thank you, sweet Jesus, for all this here good food. And thank you for blessin' us with these here good peoples. In the sweet name of Jesus, amen." As Mrs. Witherspoon lowered her hands, she invited each of us to pick up a plate and start down the line of food.

With a full plate, I walked to a folding chair at one of the tables and sat down. The chairs around me filled with Gee's Bend residents as Ned, Judy, and Arnie sat down close by. Small talk about the car trip and weather led to questions about Gee's Bend. The incredible story of survival, learned from the very people who'd lived it, began in soft, almost melodic, tones. I was completely drawn in as different voices, deeply awash in rural Southern dialect, took up the harrowing narrative.

Named after Joseph Gee, a landowner from South Carolina, Gee's Bend is an isolated section of land surrounded on three sides by an immense, miles-long bend in the Alabama River. Gee established a cotton plantation on this river land in 1816 with his slaves. In 1845, the slaves and plantation were sold to Mark Pettway, and many community residents still carry the Pettway surname.

As the crow flies, Gee's Bend is only seven miles from the county seat of Camden, Alabama. The catch was that the sole way across the good-size river to Camden was a makeshift ferry operating only when weather and the white political system in Camden permitted it—which wasn't often. The single road in and out of Gee's Bend to Alberta, the one we had used earlier in the day, was often clouded with dust in dry weather and usually thick in mud in the rainy season. The land route to Alberta and then by state road to Camden was more than forty miles, one way. So important access to the county seat to deal with all sorts of legal issues for residents was indeed a difficult and sometimes perilous journey, even if one had motorized transportation.

It is understandable why, after emancipation, the majority of freed slaves remained on Gee's Bend land, living as sharecroppers for close to a century. Little or no contact with the outside world strengthened the draconian sharecropper system that continued to enslave these isolated folks in insidious ways. For the next sixty or seventy years, stories of landowner abuse and greed were horrendous. And there seemed to be absolutely no way for residents of Gee's Bend to throw off this second oppressive yoke.

At this point in the story, our dinner hosts tossed several small, round, well-worn, coin-like pieces onto the table. We were told the wooden tokens were cruel reminders from a particularly horrific time. Some of our hosts were young adults when this stunningly tragic part of the story had occurred. Looking into faces around the room, I could see that the years had not lessened the appalling memories of that time. Holding one of these historic pieces in my hand made my skin crawl as the narrative continued.

The residents explained that, after emancipation, Gee's Bend sharecroppers were routinely issued this "funny money," as these wooden coins were called, in full payment for the farm goods and farm animals that they sold at the end of each season to the merchant who also owned the land. This illegal currency was the sole proof of each family's income. The merchant/landowner was the one and only exchange market for them, making "funny money" the only currency these families possessed. No legal US currency was ever part of the business transactions with the merchant. And living in overwhelmingly isolated circumstances, there was no other contact with any legitimate system of fair trade. Further, anything and everything these sharecroppers needed, such as basic necessities or farm-related goods like seeds or tools, could only be purchased at the local merchant's store with "funny money." Finally, any and all purchases were priced according to the merchant's whim. This intolerable rigging of financial matters pushed sharecroppers into continually oppressive debt. Income never came close to covering obligations from purchases in the store, which were always tallied up by the merchant himself.

In the summer of 1932, the merchant died. That autumn, his family arbitrarily claimed that the "funny money" no longer had value. The merchant's widow, a cruel white woman, announced that only US currency would be accepted in payment for the debts the sharecroppers owed—and all debts were being called in. Having no US currency, the entire community was left destitute.

Then the merchant's widow hired thugs to take forcible repayment of what she considered to be the sharecroppers' arrears.

Starting in Camden, her group of henchmen crossed over the Alabama River to Gee's Bend by ferry. On horseback, they entered the Gee's Bend community carrying pistols. And within a few hours, everything not nailed down was confiscated. The liquidated goods from sixty-eight black farms and households were loaded onto the ferry and floated off—personal belongings, food, livestock, seeds, everything. The community was left with absolutely nothing.

Had it not been for the Red Cross during the winter of 1932–33, the people of Gee's Bend would all have starved to death, and many still did. The National Guard was called in to help distribute foodstuffs that were shipped to the Camden armory, then ferried on occasion to Gee's Bend, which offered small but inadequate help.

By this point in the story, our church meal was almost finished, except for several large plates of sweet potato pie. Sitting in the glowing warmth of the potbellied stove, I tried to grapple with the stunning horror of the narrative. Having the real-life participants of this drama sitting in front of me brought the account amazingly to life. I had lost all interest in the pies, and everything else going on around me, as the story went on.

Starting in 1933, hope for survivors in the Gee's Bend community came in slow ways, thanks to FDR's New Deal agencies. First, much of the merchant's land was eventually sold to the federal government, and as a result, a farmers' co-op called Gee's Bend Farms, Inc. was eventually created. Some farmers received twenty acres of land and a mule to be a part of the co-op. A little later, the government finally sold tracts of land to community families on long-term payback agreements. This gave black families a bit more control over their own destinies—a rare development at that time.

The story continued up to current times. Our dinner hosts followed the extraordinary account by telling of uncommon acts of courage and bravery since the fateful years of the early '30s. Finally, they told us with enormous pride of Dr. Martin Luther King Jr.'s visit to the community just months prior. King's visit seemed to provide hope to our hosts that the Gee's Bend saga, a truly courageous story of struggle for racial equality in the Deep South, would not be forgotten but be authentically included in civil rights history.

For a few moments, I tried to sort all this out in my mind. Somehow, I was finding it hard to believe that I was actually sitting there in such a sacred meeting place—a place where, for well over a century, residents had endured injustice, indifference, greed, violence, and hatred heaped on them by folks of my race. Yet these same people, full of dignity and grace, were sharing their story and their thoughtfully prepared food with me, all out of generous love. I was incredibly humbled in the face of what felt like miraculous forgiveness. The tension dissipated, and I slowly leaned back in my chair. My mind began to swirl, questioning how I had ended up in this remarkably unnerving place called Gee's Bend.

As things were wrapping up, Mrs. Witherspoon stood and began speaking to the group again. She laid out plans for the following day. And to my surprise, after sharing the schedule details, she graciously offered each of us visitors accommodations in community homes for the night. Then Ned, Arnie, Judy, and I gathered in a spot away from the others to talk about the generous offer.

As it turned out, Judy felt strongly that we should return to a little motel in Alberta, eighteen miles away, to spend the night. Out of fear of the Ku Klux Klan coming after us if we stayed in homes of black families in this remote area, she believed the trip to Alberta was the better choice. Her suspicions brought me instant fear. I had not considered that possibility at all. So with very little consideration, and a great deal of fear, I quickly and unequivocally agreed with her thought.

I have long since regretted how this decision must have seemed to our hosts—at best ill-mannered and at worst cowardly and racist. I've never been proud of choosing to spend the night in a less-than-pristine, skuzzy little motel in Alberta over a clean bed with an extraordinary Gee's Bend family. Because of that decision, I now—what seems to be light-years later—believe without a shadow of a doubt I lost out on what would have been a particularly treasured piece of this Gee's Bend experience.

The next morning, however, we returned early on the long, winding road. Mrs. Witherspoon and Francis greeted us on the steps of the church, and once again, we found ourselves at a rickety table in the old sacred structure, this time with hot coffee and warm, homemade breakfast rolls set out in front of us.

Around the steaming coffee cups and the lovely odor of pine logs burning in the stove, the morning conversation began with another slice of Gee's Bend history: quilt making. Mrs. Witherspoon, dressed in a threadbare, simple cotton dress and a heavy, well-worn knit sweater, had pulled her salt-and-pepper hair back into a small, neat roll around the base of her neck. Her Gee's Bend quilt story started in the 1800s. She told us how her forefathers had arrived in this less-temperate climate from South Carolina when the owner moved his slave possessions to this river land. They very soon discovered a desperate need for more substantial bedcovers—as none had been provided against the cold of central Alabama winters. In response, nurturing slave women started piecing together strips of cloth—old rags, worn-out clothing, whatever scraps of fabric they could get their hands on. This activity became communal, perhaps inspired by dearly treasured shreds of African textiles that had literally come on the backs of slaves on the horrendous slave ship journeys. A distinct style of piecing together these fragments of cloth developed over time. The glorious results turned out to be practical yet artistically extraordinary bed quilts.

So it was early on that cold January morning that we were escorted out of the church and guided to the other large building in the community clearing. Mrs. Witherspoon, a small-framed woman in sturdy low-heeled black shoes, shepherded us into a commercial-looking, metal-clad structure. A sign outside proudly proclaimed "Freedom Quilting Bee." There, we became firsthand witnesses to how those fantastic pieces of quilt art were actually created.

Walking in, the acrid smell of burning wood radiated with warmth from the potbellied stove glowing nearby. Great piles of brightly colored cloth pieces were scattered around on the floor. Situated on a solid platform near these piles sat two humongous wooden quilt frames. Stretched across each frame was an eye-catching, semifinished quilt. Three community women dressed much like Mrs. Witherspoon were industriously bent over the frames, each one demonstrating the challenging hand-quilting process. A sense of enormous pride radiated from the women.

The feeling connected with a place in my psyche housing memories of my grandmother—a woman who'd sown beautiful slipcovers and curtains for a well-established interior decorator. As a small girl, I had been enchanted with the richly hued, textured fabrics she always had on hand. I was continually encouraged to touch, feel, and admire the yards and piles of lovely textiles around her workspace. So those amazing semifinished quilts in the Gee's Bend Freedom Quilting Bee building made me feel as though, in a sense, I belonged there, too.

We all sat down on old wooden folding chairs and became entranced by the quilting activity. To my surprise, Francis joined in to tell us the next chapter of the quilt story. His Southern voice, tinged with humor, explained how, as part of his civil rights work for SIP, he had recently been driving on the rural back roads of an isolated nearby community, Possum Bend. After a time, he found himself clearly lost and disoriented. Stopping to collect his thoughts, he looked around and noticed a clothesline hanging low with three richly colored bed quilts. He was completely taken in by the colorful designs. He knew he had to find whomever the pieces belonged to, but when Francis went looking for the owner, she ran away in fear. We were told that fear was common for residents of the area when white people came seeking them out. History had shown residents that no good thing usually came from any interaction with unknown white folks in the Bend communities. Mrs. McDaniels, the owner of the quilts, was no different.

Somehow with persistence, though, Francis was able to find Mrs. McDaniels. After working to establish trust, Francis learned that her quilts were products of an enterprise comprised entirely of local women. Their collective effort had been supplying their community with warm bed coverings for a very long time. But something clicked in Francis's imagination, and he saw the quilts as possible unique folk-art creations. Francis was struck with the idea that perhaps there might be a market outside of the community for the astonishing pieces. He contemplated how an organized quilt-marketing endeavor could possibly result in bettering the lives financially of the community.

During our visit, Francis was in the process of helping to strategize a long-range business endeavor known as the Freedom Quilting Bee. Because of this work, the magnificent quilts would eventually become famous nationally and, to everyone's amazement, even achieve acclaim around the world, finding permanent homes in world-renowned museums. As I write this story nearly fifty years later, these textile treasures are considered exceptional in improvisational design and geometric simplicity. But on that cold day in 1967, Gee's Bend quilts had not yet achieved anything like national acclaim. As I sat there watching the fascinating handwork on the quilts, I had little idea of how the lives of the women in front of me would be changed for the better as their beautiful masterpieces would grow in value in the months and years ahead.

But the quilt-making building was not the last stop on our consciousness-raising experience that day. There was one last, hands-on chapter in the Gee's Bend tour for us. After leaving the Freedom Quilting Bee building, we crunched our way through layers of dried pine needles strewn over hard-packed dirt to one of the many smaller dwellings. The structures, randomly covered with varying lengths of wood pieces cobbled together under odd strips of tar paper, sat slightly askew amid towering pine trees.

The one we headed for was facing the church, with a slightly off-balance pitched roof. On one edge of the roof, a chimney sat with precarious abandon. Two rickety steps accessed a tiny front porch. We followed our intrepid tour guide, Mrs. Witherspoon, up the steps and through the front door. There we found ourselves graciously welcomed into the home of Mr. and Mrs. Witherspoon.

Mrs. Witherspoon was proud as can be of her home as she led us through the immaculate living area and miniscule kitchen. Six children had been raised in the compact space. A small tattered black-and-white photograph of the family, from when the children were young, was hung in a conspicuous spot on the wall.

But behind the photograph, the walls of the home were an amazing sight. Layers and layers of newspaper and magazine pages had been glued on top of each other across each wall to function as inexpensive insulation. The startling overall appearance was a montage of abstract art. Each visible newspaper or magazine picture had been carefully chosen to occupy that particular place. Some showed headlines, such as Eisenhower being elected president and the assignation of JFK. Some showed pictures of white women posing in expensive high-fashion clothes from *Vogue* magazine. The variety of headlines and photos was stunning. Floor to ceiling, the walls were thickly covered. Then, as a final step in the wall covering process, after everything had dried, a knife was used to cut around each door and window opening, and the window sections had been carefully removed. It was an extremely practical way to insulate the fragile, thin-walled dwelling. And the whole scene came with the lovely additional benefit of providing intense visual interest in the room. Looking around, my eyes hardly knew where to stop.

From the main living area, Mrs. Witherspoon showed us into the two bedrooms in the back of the house. In each of the two rooms, rather dilapidated-looking dressers stood in corners while iron bed frames were covered with more spectacular handmade quilts. It was remarkable to see the quilts in the exact places they were supposed to occupy.

It was clear to me that life had been anything but easy in Gee's Bend, as the tour inside the Witherspoon home demonstrated. But I was struck by the preponderance of color and design that filled the community in the most unexpected places. And to me, those demonstrations were profound signs of eternal, unquenchable hope.

That afternoon Arnie, Judy, Ned, and I climbed back into the car, sharing goodbyes with Francis and the community residents. As Arnie drove us back down the long roadway to Alberta, and then on to Mobile, a rerun of the past two days sped through my head. I wasn't sure how to process everything. I felt almost as though the whole experience might even have been a dream. Sitting in the car as it raced down the road, I couldn't yet begin to understand how powerfully the experience had touched my belief system, but somewhere deep, I knew I had been changed.

CHAPTER EIGHT

Mardi Gras

Mobile, with its wonderful assortment of historic places dating back to antebellum times and even earlier, was growing on me. I was fascinated to learn Spanish explorers sailed into Mobile Bay as early as 1500. Mobile's Mardi Gras, the oldest carnival celebration in the United States, started in 1703, just one year after the new settlement was recognized as the capital of colonial French Louisiana. Passing from France to Spain and then into British hands over early years, Mobile maintains amazing threads of each country's presence, even today. Finding out more about this rich history was an exciting pastime for Ned and me.

Because Mobile took tremendous pride as the home of the first Mardi Gras celebration in the United States, the event was a huge tradition. Ned and I arrived in September, and by Mardi Gras time in March, I was excited and impatient to see for myself what all the talk was about. The stories surrounding the celebration were told and retold at almost every social activity we attended, so I could hardly wait for the upcoming Mardi Gras bash.

Mardi Gras was experienced in two ways: one was attending large, noisy street parades each night during the few weeks preceding Ash Wednesday, and the second was attending formal dress balls or dances hosted by private mystic Mardi Gras societies, who happened to be the same groups responsible for the nightly public parades. The extravagant dress balls were private affairs requiring formal invitations from society members, while the nightly parades were a chance for anyone and everyone to be a part of the carnival fun.

Soon after arriving in Mobile, Ned and I began spending time with new congregation friends, Louie and Margie Ittmann. Being with the Ittmann family for informal meals and holidays became a comfortable arrangement. Louie and Margie had a teenage daughter, Nancy; a young adult son, Robbie; and Louie's mother, a happy New Orleans expat, all living under the same roof. Spending time with the Ittmann clan made me feel like I was with my happy family.

Louie happened to be a member of one of the private Mardi Gras societies—or "crews," as they are sometimes called—and to our good fortune, Louie invited us to a Mardi Gras ball sponsored by his private crew. So we would not only get to see parades firsthand, we would also get to actually dance at a Mardi Gras ball. And I, for one, was eagerly looking forward to it.

Growing up in a narrow, pious religious system meant that, for me, smoking and taking part in other "worldly pleasures" such as alcohol and dancing were forbidden. The invitation to Louie's Mardi Gras ball gave me a great opportunity to throw open the windows and move beyond my strict religious upbringing into a newly burgeoning sense of self. Being married to a man I adored, who clearly espoused a less-uptight view of life, pushed me into letting go of the fundamentalist ways of viewing the world. I no longer believed I was defined as a Christian by a moralistic list of judgmental behaviors I piously avoided while I actively proselytized for the group. Instead, the notion of Christianity had become trying to live out the life Jesus had modeled—a life of love, justice, and mercy. So, as if right on cue, the Mardi Gras ball came along at a wonderful internal transition in my life.

I found it great fun to get my head around what to wear for the very formal Mardi Gras ball. Margie and I both enjoyed home sewing, and so together we worked on my outfit. I splurged at a local fabric store on a luscious piece of ivory brocade to make a beautiful floor-length pencil skirt. I already owned a perfect sleeveless, beaded ivory top, lined in lightweight silk. I was certain that pairing the pieces would give me the ideal outfit. Ned rented his requisite formal attire—white tie and tails.

The day of the ball, I fixed my hair with an extra-poufy crown section. My special new skirt and top, combined with cream satin heels, made me feel simply elegant—almost like Jackie O.

In the naiveté of our youth, Ned and I showed up at the Mobile Public Auditorium the night of the ball feeling as though we looked quite smashing. Entering the otherwise mundane space of the venue, we were amazed to see the whole place magically transformed with gigantic, ornate fake Greek columns, huge fabric swaths of gold taffeta everywhere, and tons of super-tall stylized vases filled with an array of extravagant fresh orchids, azaleas, camellias, and gardenias. The humdrum public space had been miraculously turned into a fairyland setting, and it momentarily took my breath away.

I felt so proud walking in on Ned's arm. We quickly found Louie and Margie, and the four of us walked around enjoying the scene for a bit. Finally, we sat down at one of the gold-taffeta-covered tables with classy white wrought-iron chairs situated near the big dance floor. Dressed in white tie and tails, and with his wonderfully easy way of throwing back his head and letting go with enormous bursts of laughter, Louie made us feel completely welcome and at ease. And Margie, too—who looked sensational in a glamorous midnight-blue satin ball gown, intricately decorated with rhinestones at the scooped neckline—was welcoming with her cheerful banter.

At the far end of the room sat a large orchestra, each musician dressed in full tie and tails. I had never seen such formal opulence. I found myself breathing in a feeling of happy abandon. Gone were the "shoulds" and "should nots" of my youth. The loud, engaging music mix wove together big band favorites like "Pennsylvania 6-5000" and "The Last Time I Saw Paris" with contemporary tunes like "I'm a Believer." The sounds resonated to every corner of the rafters, and the whole building shook with energy.

Along one wall, enormous tables were laden with large platters of fried oysters, shrimp, crawdads, steak, pulled pork, and fried chicken, along with a wide array of salads, finger foods, and sweets. At the bar, you could order any concoction you might want to drink. The intoxicating sent of gardenias was beautiful as Louie and Ned went off to the bar for some decadent things for the four of us to drink.

Then, for a quick moment, my mind went to an intensely familiar spot. I thought, *What is a staid Northern Baptist girl, whose family and childhood religion eschew this kind of debauchery, doing in this place dressed like this?* But almost as quickly as the thought came to me, that niggling voice was silenced by the sight of my handsome, smiling husband standing next to me with his hand outstretched, offering me a turn on the dance floor. I stood up excitedly, thinking, *Look out world, here we come.* His hand securely held my arm as he guided me to the open floor. What happened next was right out of the dream machine—he gathered me in his arms, and we began to move around like a for-real dancing couple. I felt a transformation happening instantly. Dancing with Ned's arm around me in the middle of that gorgeous scene seemed almost too perfect. I allowed the sophisticated image of this young woman—who believed the world was her oyster and who was married to this promising, confident young man—to roll over me. And it felt good.

You see, beneath all the hoopla, deep down in a secret place, I'd cultivated this sophisticated-young-woman image because it conjured up the picture of myself as the wife of a man successfully on the move, career wise. In this dream, I nurtured a future of fine, middle-class privilege as the wife of a charismatic minister. I told myself that the Mardi Gras ball was only a taste of the amazing things that were to come for us. I had worked toward achieving this kind of dream all through college, and I just felt like I belonged to this way of life. But I had no way of knowing just how misguided that image would actually turn out to be for me.

Besides the ball, there was another side to the Mardi Gras experience. Louie built on the magic of the ball by also bringing Ned and me into the fascinating world of brash Mardi Gras parades.

Each night for several days before the beginning of Lent, members of these historic mystic crews organized public parades. In costume and masks, members tossed "throws" from gigantic, colorfully decorated floats to people lined up along the parade route. These "throws" included plastic bead necklaces, fake doubloon coins, candy, and small yummy plastic-wrapped treats known as moon pies. New to Ned and me, those infamous moon pies, a true Southern delicacy, were two round graham cracker cookies with marshmallow filling in the center, dipped in a chocolate coating. The ultimate parade success story was to have several moon pie packets in your take-home bag after the parade ended. And on the night of Louie's crew parade, he knew just where Ned and I were standing along the parade route. Weaving around happily on the float, Louie made sure his fellow society celebrants threw a goodly number of Mardi Gras parade treasures our way, especially moon pies. It was super fun, indeed.

The most memorable of these parades was on the evening of Fat Tuesday. This, the last parade of the Mardi Gras season, had some unique features. All the parade floats were pulled by mules—instead of motorized vehicles. And to add to the overall sense of antiquity, the parade began after dark with several men dressed in short brown robe-like costumes over dark pants with rope belts. Each group of two or three escorts walked together next to the floats carrying huge, flaming torches to light the scene. The eerie feeling that we had somehow stepped back a hundred years or so permeated the streets as we watched the flames and shadows slowly float past us. I had never seen a reenactment of history before like the one in front of me. And after that magical carnival parade, I realized the spell of historic Mardi Gras—Mobile style—had captured my psyche, too. The audacious experience added heft to my growing acceptance of this city as my home.

My Mardi Gras story does not end there, however. Some thirty years later, I was working for Los Angeles Unified School District when I crossed paths with another central office employee who also had firsthand knowledge of the enchantment of a Mobile Mardi Gras. Dr. Mary Ramirez, a beautiful, brilliant, and thoroughly delightful coworker, who happened to be black, told me she'd grown up in Mobile. The special part of her story was that, years after my husband and I had left Mobile, she had been chosen to be queen of one of the Mobile Mardi Gras black celebrations.

You see, the Mardi Gras productions I participated in were, and still are, racially segregated. Early on, the black community's response to white Mardi Gras was to develop thriving and spectacular all-black Mardi Gras events. And one of these black occasions was the venue where my friend had been celebrated as queen.

In 1967, I was brain-dead to the fact these private events were racially segregated. I had floated around in my wonderful, privileged dreams on the dance floor that night thinking things were just as they should be. It never even occurred to me that all the ball attendees were white. I was happy in my smug complacency, immersed in a culture of mainstream racism. My worldview was to change dramatically before too long, but on that night, I was caught in the flow.

So I was grateful for my friend Mary, whose friendship lovingly reminded me again of the deep, insidious racial divide in this country. I realized one more time how easy it is to accept the status quo as normal and right, as I had that night in Mobile.

CHAPTER NINE

Dog River Dock

Ned and I had been growing more and more content with our lives inside the comfortable church community. We socialized with church members frequently and felt as though we had been accepted into the church bubble with few reservations. An unwritten rule for being a good church member seemed to include the expectation that you invited the pastor and his wife to dinner. Going often to homes of members helped Ned and me get to know people quickly. The added bonus of seeing folks in their own homes was that it contributed substantially to the narrative of each member for us.

Without intentionally discussing racial matters in any of these social settings, or in any church-related get-togethers, Ned and I felt pretty sure we understood where most of the congregation members were coming from on those issues. Offhand disparaging remarks like "Martin Luther King Jr. is really a Communist after all" were common in the white community. In his pastoral capacity, Ned had cautiously taken on social gospel issues in sermons and newsletters, especially racial equality topics, from the beginning. And the few members who connected with this agenda verbally shared with Ned how much they supported his efforts. Those who didn't support this agenda remained fairly quiet. That is, until one steamy Saturday afternoon in early spring 1968.

Over the past few years throughout the South, civil rights protesters had been harassed, beaten, and even killed. Although white community leaders in Mobile attempted to portray the city as more tolerant to racial matters, the truth was that Mobile had kept only an unstable lid on overt civil disobedience demonstrations. The prevailing attitude, which politicians attempted to keep under wraps, saw racially motivated civil unrest as a basic threat to the way of life most white residents enjoyed. The culturally accepted white power structure was seriously challenged by the notion of racial equality. It was Governor George Wallace's state, after all. Wallace, the Alabama governor who just five years earlier had proudly proclaimed to huge, cheering audiences: "segregation now, segregation tomorrow, and segregation forever." Strong feelings supporting this brand of bigotry had not lessened in Alabama in the following five years. And although the public messaging from the city of Mobile attempted to tell a different tale, underneath, most citizens were no different in their racial feelings than those from any other part of the state, or the South in general.

On that early spring day, church members Billy John Skrims and his wife, Bernice, had invited us for a good ol' Southern barbeque at their home near scenic Dog River. The invitation was Billy John and Bernice's effort at meeting the church member expectation of entertaining the pastor and his wife. But not only had we been invited to the Skrims home for a cookout, there was the added bonus of a cruise on Billy John's boat. I was especially excited about that part of the invitation because I had always loved the frequent mini fishing trips on Lake Erie each summer with my dad, mother, and sister. Trying to contend with hot, humid spurts in the weather, my dad would rent a small boat in the evening hours, and we would float around languidly on the cool lake—fishing pole and line dangling over the edge of the craft. Although the boats my dad would rent for our family excursions on Lake Erie were little more than overgrown rowboats, Billy John's vessel, which he proudly owned outright, was a for-real yacht—small but nonetheless a yacht. Life seemed to be improving for me.

Arriving late morning, Ned and I made efforts to appear properly attired for a personal visit to a member's home. Ned was in casual black cotton slacks paired with a plaid short-sleeved shirt, and I wore khaki Bermuda shorts and a sleeveless white cotton blouse and comfortable tennis shoes. We were especially aware that this outing happened to be with one of the church's most influential members. Billy John owned a beautiful tract of waterfront land on Dog River with a boat dock where his snazzy yacht was tied up. The home, extremely spacious for two adults, was designed to allow its inhabitants to spend the maximum amount of time enjoying water views from several comfy, screened-in spots around the rambling perimeter. The plan for the day seemed to be lunch followed by a leisurely cruise on the yacht, named the *Bernice Doll.*

The Skrimses displayed a tad of edginess as we said hello, and I wasn't sure what the cause for this was. Maybe they were uncomfortable because they were almost old enough to be our parents, or maybe their die-hard Southerner loyalties caused them to mistrust us, or perhaps a combination of both, who knows. Ned and I sometimes felt our Northern roots put us at a disadvantage in social settings in Mobile, but there was nothing we could do to change that basic formula. The church knew who we were when the job was offered to Ned.

After the pork barbeque lunch with all the trimmings, Bernice and I ended up seated on chairs in the screened front porch trying to cool off with big glasses of heavily sweetened ice tea. The air had the familiar whiff of rotten eggs I had become accustomed to and was heavy with humidity. White wrought-iron furniture pieces were scattered around the rather grand space. Each pillow and seat cushion was covered with stiff avocado-colored plastic vinyl, making sitting a rather uncomfortable experience. To add to the awkwardness, I could hear rather rude, crunchy noises as weight was cautiously relocated on the cushions. Despite the distractions,

I was certain the whole outdoor set had cost Billy John a fairly sizeable sum. The entire picture of house, land, dock, and boat was quite something, indeed. But it had the feeling of "new" money— money that had not been in the family for generations. This clamoring sense of wealth appeared to have a need to show how much a good ol' Southern boy who had grown up poor can now spend on himself and his family. And that's fair enough.

In white sandals, Bernice sported a pink-and-white-striped polyester shorts set with rickrack trim around the scalloped neck. She sat back comfortably, crossed her legs, ice tea in hand, and started her story. The fact she was born and raised in an impoverished Mobile family fed the pride of what she labeled her "Southern heritage." After two years in high school, at the age of sixteen, Bernice had quit school and married Billy John. Small framed and a bit plump, Bernice walked with exaggerated effort from an arthritic hip. I shared with her how I admired her curly salt-and-pepper hair cut short in a flattering style. She responded with a pleasant giggle, losing a bit of her uptightness. Talking more about herself, she told me in a deep molasses accent that she had happily found her life's purpose as housewife, mother, and now grandmother. She especially liked the fact that her married life had been comfortable due to Billy John's financial success. Her dreams had come true. And Bernice believed it was due to hard work, being such good people, and following the prescribed mores of the current political system. My take was that those mores were perhaps based on a completely unequal racial system, but I kept the notion to myself and continued to listen to her story.

Since beginning my job as a caseworker for the county, I had consciously begun to look at everyday situations with different eyes. So in my estimation, Bernice had been fortunate in marrying a man who'd had reliable work at the Mobile shipyards over the years. She had never had to worry about providing basic necessities for herself or her three children. Billy John started as an entry-level shipyard worker and quickly moved up the ladder into a position in the upper echelons of employees at the shipyards. Bernice had really lived a rather charmed life. In the words of my sweet grandmother, Bernice had "arrived." She was of a mind to see Billy John and herself as more than entitled to all they had acquired as good, hard-working white folks. And from what I could see, they had acquired a good deal. I just wasn't so sure a man with a different skin color would have had the same basic opportunities to climb the career ladder as Billy John had.

As we continued our talk, Billy John shouted to us from the dock, "Come on down here, y'all. We're getting' ready to go."

The yacht was inviting, and we easily climbed aboard as Billy John loosened the ropes. The *Bernice Doll* was bedecked with a fine wide yellow-and-white-striped interior design. It sparkled under the hot sun. Settling in for the cruise was great fun, with Billy John popping on his skipper hat.

We headed languidly down Dog River toward Mobile Bay, enjoying the semitropical scenery in what seemed to me to be sheer luxury. When we reached the wide mouth of the river, Billy John maneuvered the craft into the sparkling waters of the bay. The breezes were wonderfully cooling, and we picked up a bit of speed as we headed down to Dauphin Island. Billy John was as proud as he could be when we reached the island. He was intent on showing us the beach house he owned there. The house was one in a line of, for me, unusual-looking dwellings, each propped up on several long, leggy stilts designed to limit exposure to high ocean waves. The whole picture looked as if it had been reproduced from a scene right out of a tropical movie set, and I was taken in completely. Billy John had certainly proved beyond a shadow of any doubt that he was a financial success.

Mr. Billy John Skrims was, of course, the star of the day. As the afternoon slowly faded into early evening, we returned from our magical cruise back to his Dog River home. It had been a wonderfully memorable experience.

At the end of the boat ride, we climbed out of the *Bernice Doll* and onto the dock. It was then, as we were preparing to leave, that Billy John dropped the bombshell. Six foot tall, in his late fifties with thinning gray hair and a barrel-shaped silhouette, Billy John's statements were always made with great certainty. He knew the trademark braggadocio behavior he exhibited always brought him welcome attention. As Billy John tied up the boat, he pulled his tall frame upright and stretched his arm out straight, smugly pointing to the property adjacent to his on the river. "See that ol' piece of land over there?" he said loudly to us, smiling broadly, and waving his hand in the air. "It was up for sale awhile back, and I'll be doggone, I had to end up buyin' it. Yep . . . know why?" And then after a short pause, he boldly continued, "'Cause I don't want no n***** boy buyin' it up." Then with a deep guttural laugh, he went on, "Sure don't want no n***** neighbors 'round here."

Billy John spoke the words with incredible confidence. He seemed to have the unaccountably astonishing notion that Ned and I were both dues-paying members of his bigoted, racist club— as though we were complicit in his rhetoric. His words seemed predicated on the notion of his position in the church—he was, after all, the biggest donor by far in the congregation. Somehow, he seemed to believe that entitled him to say any hateful thing he wanted to his pastor. If Ned ever thought he had any influence over changing racial attitudes of his parishioners, that moment proved him utterly and completely wrong.

Ned and I were both speechless. Electricity shot through the air as our eyes were drawn to each other defensively. The word "n*****" completely unnerved me—I had only ever heard the word used in the disgusting rhetoric of white supremacists. But in this private church-family gathering, the horrible sting of it filled the air with a nauseating stench. Our shock over hearing Billy John's words left us in total disarray.

But we were both thoroughly enmeshed in the basic cultural tenant our families had taught us: always behave with decency and respect in someone else's house and never, never cause a scene. Here we were in a situation dominated by our generous and powerful host. Further, Ned was in the sticky relationship of employer-employee. So instead of immediately confronting Billy John's hateful intolerance, Ned and I just quickly gathered our things. We said little besides a polite thank-you and goodbye, pretending as though nothing had just happened. Then dazed, we headed for the car.

As I think back on the whole incident, I'm not sure if Billy John or Bernice were aware that anything inappropriate had even happened, but I can't say for sure. Ned and I were both just trying to grapple with the audaciousness of the situation while trying not to cause any impolite disruption—good manners, you know. Ned was also caught in the dilemma of knowing that his job as pastor was in no small part dependent on the approval of this man. So the question of how much confrontation he was willing to risk kept gnawing at him.

I kept thinking that I couldn't have really heard what Billy John had actually said. The words continued spinning in my head—"n***** boy"? Had he really said "n***** boy"? I found myself sitting in the front seat of the car in a state of shock. Ned's face was pulled into a tight, angry scowl—each body movement had an extraordinary jerkiness to it. Driving off, excessively fast, it was clear Ned was about as incensed as I had ever seen him.

It took a good long time pacing around at home for Ned to start to calm down. Billy John's comments had forced Ned to look inside and blame himself for his ineffectiveness as a pastor. He felt like he had made absolutely no progress changing human values in congregation members, if that incident were any indication.

The infamous day on the Dog River boat dock marked a drastic change in my relationship with church members, too. I became much less trusting and open in church settings. It was as if I had donned a symbolic flap jacket to cover exposed places in my psyche, and for me, the jacket created an unsettling sense of discomfort. I was beginning to think that all was not as wonderful for me in Mobile as I had thought it was. My thick coating of naiveté was beginning to crack.

Billy John's comments had an even deeper effect on my husband, though. This episode motivated Ned to promote racial equality agendas in his pastoral work no matter where it led. And it should be no surprise to anyone that Ned's more focused racial equality commitment did not bode well for the stability of our lives together in Mobile.

CHAPTER TEN

A Gathering Storm

I believe racism permeates the cultural air we breathe. It seems to me, stereotypes that usually promote racism are a bit akin to poisonous vines growing invasively in our heads despite our best intentions to be grounded in the soil of compassion and reason. I think the following narrative from my experience with another church member speaks to one of the insidious ways bigotry slides into a person's psyche. But what is even more insidious is the cowardly avoidance of the spectacle of bigotry, as my reactions are only too willing to demonstrate in this story.

Callie, a young mother in our congregation, was raised in northern Illinois in a decent Christian home that certainly did not publicly wear the badge of racism. She married John, a man she had met as a student at a local university and who now worked for Scott Paper Company as a highly paid product technician. This white couple in their early thirties—transplants from the North about five years earlier—owned a large and quite comfortable home in a beautiful part of Mobile where they lived with their three small children. Thriving in the role she had been blessed with, Callie was a stay-at-home mom, a devoted member of Holy

Cross Lutheran Church, and a so-called model Christian—to her friends, at least.

The economic reality of life in Mobile allowed for quite gracious living on a relatively modest income. The cost of living in Mobile was below the national average. So a daily housemaid, which would be an extravagance in other parts of the country, was for the most part considered not even much of a luxury for a large slice of economically comfortable families in Mobile. As was always the case, black labor was cheap, and day maids were black. It was not surprising, then, that many financially solid families in our congregation had maids to take care of cooking tasks, housecleaning, childcare, and laundry, usually all for the low price of about five dollars a day, out of which the maid paid her own transportation costs.

Callie, too, had her own household maid, as she happily embraced the Southern style of rather grand living. But appreciation for the wonderful gift of low-cost household help often got lost in the tedium of day-to-day living. In my small circle, I was continually surprised by how these day maids were targeted in a number of demeaning ways. I often overheard disgusting stereotypes of these hardworking females in the market, at church events, and at other social gatherings. Offhand insensitive and cruel comments regarding these women were pejoratively thrown about, having to do with their laziness, shiftlessness, dishonesty, and ignorance.

The truth was that these day workers had exceedingly difficult lives. Little opportunity for education, absolutely no family resources, and dreadful living conditions marinated together to destroy any real hope for ever getting beyond their current state of affairs despite continual hard work. These women were worn down to a nubbin, living courageous lives in a system that did not work for them whatsoever. Each day was daunting. They would leave their own children at home early in the morning to take public transportation or walk, often miles, to get to work to care for white people's children and homes. All the while, the white kids they cared for lived a fairy-tale existence compared to their own black children. So at a Holy Cross dinner one Sunday evening when Callie rather proudly told others and me about how she had to fire her "shiftless and dishonest" maid, I was taken aback.

The story went like this. Callie had been away from the house most of the day leaving Yvette, her maid, alone in the house with her children. Yvette had children of her own at home that her elderly, ailing grandmother was left to care for while she was the housekeeper/nanny for Callie's family. Yvette often found herself without enough money after a full week of work to even put enough food on the table, much less buy clothes, school supplies, or other basic necessities for her own family. Her husband, Richard, worked wherever and however he could, only now and again. He could not begin to match her five-dollar-a-day income with whatever job he could find, but he continued to try nonetheless. So Yvette was the primary breadwinner.

On the birthday of Yvette's young daughter, the maid had lamented to herself that she had no gift or even a birthday cake for her own child. Not surprising, then, knowing that Callie, her employer, was going to be away for several more hours, Yvette took a box of cake mix from Callie's well-stocked kitchen pantry. She quickly made a birthday cake from the packaged mix for her small daughter. Then she mixed ingredients for frosting and hurriedly covered the cake with the sticky stuff. At least she would have a for-real birthday cake for her own little one, she thought. The excitement must have thrilled her, but underneath she had to be deeply worried about being found out.

The next part of the drama for Yvette was how to get the cake safely home without Callie finding out what she had done. So Yvette carefully wrapped the cake in aluminum foil and took the treasure out back to the garbage cans. After looking around to see if she was being watched, she precisely deposited the aluminum-foil-wrapped cake in a garbage pail. Then she put the remnants of the day's cooking over the top of the carefully wrapped cake and secured the garbage can cover.

The plan unraveled when Yvette secretly returned that evening to try to claim the prize cake from the garbage. Unfortunately, Callie saw Yvette when she came back and confronted her about the deceit. Remembering the stereotypes of day-maid dishonesty that Callie had heard again and again, she responded by telling Yvette she was fired, and no, she could not take the pathetic cake home to her daughter because of course "that would be stealing."

For me, the remarkable part of this decidedly uncompassionate tale was how smugly Callie told it as we sat around a generous church dinner. Callie seemed to want everyone listening to know how savvy she had become to these culturally unacceptable acts perpetrated by black maids. Callie sounded quite pleased that she had found the dishonest culprit and had meted out appropriate justice. It seemed she was looking for our praise in how well she had handled the situation as she acted out the stereotype to the letter.

The parish hall had become a sort of unofficial courtroom. Hiding in my safe place of quiet, cowardly fear, I did not respond to Callie or the others. Especially as the pastor's wife, I didn't want to stir things up on racial issues. Feeling a deep hollowness inside, I sat stiffly on the uncomfortable folding chair staring blankly at Callie. I was extraordinarily sad for Yvette because I could see her face in my mind's eye as if she were one of my welfare clients again caught in the overwhelming injustice of the system in which we all lived. And I didn't believe I could do anything to change the way things worked. That was the worst of it—that feeling of helplessness. For me, this perceived religious premise of legalism, or making certain people were righteously punished for wrongdoings had, once again, outweighed the elusive Christian concept of compassion, the very essence of the life of Jesus. I kept my unacceptable thoughts stuffed safely inside, as it was clear this jury of onlookers had already decided in Callie's favor, and I didn't want to upset the status quo. But I was becoming more acutely aware of the incredible land mines in this racially charged hotbed of a place where I was living.

As racial land mines go, though, Grace Lutheran Church, the oldest Lutheran church in Alabama, would probably not be at the top of the list for most people. It sits on a prominent slice of land on Government Boulevard, the main artery in Mobile in the historic downtown section of the city. Known with great respect as the "Mother Church" in Mobile Lutheran circles, its history goes back to the nineteenth century. But its role in the list of racial land mines for us soon became clear.

In late summer of 1967, we heard that Grace Lutheran Church was going all-out to celebrate the hundredth anniversary of its founding that October. The national president of the Lutheran Church—Missouri Synod had been invited for the special service scheduled for a Sunday afternoon. In our church circles, it was going to be a very big deal, indeed.

Besides Grace Lutheran, there were two other all-white Lutheran churches in Mobile that were part of this synod or national church body. One of these was Ned's congregation, Holy Cross. Every member of the two other all-white congregations had been invited to attend the special service at Grace.

In addition to this first block of three all-white Lutheran congregations in Mobile was a second block of three Lutheran congregations, also members of the Lutheran Church—Missouri Synod. Excluding pastors and their wives, the second block was composed entirely of black members. Therefore, there were three all-white congregations and three all-black congregations in this specific brand of Lutheranism in Mobile.

In conversations between Ned and Arnie, a white pastor of one of the all-black churches, an interesting discovery was made. For two of the black congregations, the invitation to the anniversary celebration at Grace had been sent personally to the homes of their white pastors. But the invitations did not include any members of their black congregations. And as far as the third black Lutheran church went, no member, not even the black pastor, had received an invitation to the big event.

Both Arnie and Ned were taken aback by the striking difference in the invitations. Obviously, black Lutherans in the same brand of Lutheranism were being patently excluded from the big "Mother Church" event. Arnie and Ned found this difference in invitations inexcusably discriminatory against black Lutherans. Being the budding clergy activists that they were, they decided to do something to bring about change.

Fiery letters of protest were sent to Grace Lutheran Church, and to the president of the national Lutheran church body, pointing out the overt racism involved in planning the event. Additionally, Ned and Arnie made angry phone calls demanding that equality prevail. Grace Lutheran Church was urged to issue consistently open invitations for all members of the Missouri Synod churches in Mobile—black and white alike.

Thanks to the calls and protest letters, the president of the synod refused to come and be the featured speaker if all Missouri Synod church members in Mobile were not equally welcomed at the service, and so Grace Lutheran Church eventually reissued invitations to include all members from each one of the six Missouri Synod churches in Mobile.

There was one caveat, however, in the invites to the black Lutherans. Their invitations included a directive that should they choose to come, they were to be seated only in the balcony section of the church. As appalling as this appears now, at the time it felt like a small step forward nonetheless.

This victory energized Ned and Arnie, compelling them to think more actively about moving civil rights agendas within the membership of their own two churches—one all black, one all white. As close friends, Arnie and Judy often came over to our house to hang out with us on Sunday nights. It was a time for the four of us to relax in a supportive, nonjudgmental place.

Ned and Arnie would usually focus the conversations on how to contribute more to solving racial issues within the church setting. During one of these Sunday-night get-togethers over some strong ice tea, these two guys came up with the seemingly absurd idea of a biracial service between the two congregations—one that would include communion, no less. Sitting around in the comfortable air-conditioned coolness of the small living room, we all had a simply hilarious laugh thinking about the possibility of it. But then the look on Ned's and Arnie's faces turned stone-cold serious. They realized the idea was valid and that they needed to try it. Stunned, Judy and I looked at each other as though we had just touched the end of a hot wire.

So a few weeks later, after scrutinizing the church calendar for an appropriate church service that would work well for the biracial plan, the season of Lent—with its abundance of extra worship services—stood out. Discussing which one might work best, the Maundy Thursday service with Ned's home church, Holy Cross, tentatively hosting the gathering appeared to be the best choice. Both men knew the audacious plan would succeed or fail on the approval of the voter assembly of each congregation. They were also very aware that if the idea were approved, it would, without question, result in hateful racial backlash somehow.

Holding a biracial service was a very daring concept in many ways because Maundy Thursday, the Thursday immediately before Easter, is observed in the Christian Church as the major commemoration of the Last Supper, the origin of the communion or Eucharist tradition.

I fell into a worried funk. Contemplating the biracial service was almost more than my naive brain could imagine. I thought Arnie and Ned had lost their collective minds. The concept, I believed, would test the relationship between the church membership and Ned to its fullest.

What would our church members think, in the middle of increasing racial tensions, about having to sit on their own church pew next to a black person? After all, the white members of Grace Lutheran Church hadn't much liked the very same idea when planning the anniversary service in their church a few months back. But to push the concept to its surreal conclusion, how would the white members respond when asked to drink out of the same communion chalice or cup as the black guests in a common communion service? Now, as far as I was concerned, that was the final nail in this radical proposal.

All this didn't deter my husband, though. Ned didn't waste any time acting on this provocative plan. Right away, he took the idea to host a biracial service with Arnie's congregation to the church's voter assembly. This group, the main decision-making body within the church body was composed of only male church members. In most, if not all, Missouri Synod Lutheran churches, an exclusively male voter assembly was the only historically acceptable form of congregation governance. And usually, very few male voters at Holy Cross Lutheran attended the regular voter assembly meetings.

So at that first meeting, when Ned presented the biracial Maundy Thursday service, there were only a handful of men present. Amazingly to me, the biracial church service vote passed. What happened was, I think, the assorted collection of male voters who had chanced to attend that evening were shockingly overwhelmed by the idea. They did not want to look bigoted in front of their pastor, so they just passively agreed to approve the service and then quickly and quietly retreated home.

Of course, Ned was pleased with the outcome of the vote. He even felt a little vindicated after the recent incident on Billy John's boat dock. Believing he might have miscalculated, my husband now thought there were others in the congregation beyond the few he already knew about who were really supportive of racial equality issues. He had tried his best to present the idea as a demonstration of courageous Christians sending the simple message of brothers and sisters in Christ, blind to skin color, worshiping together. So Ned saw this first vote as great news, indeed, not realizing how out of touch he might really be.

Then the backlash set in. It didn't take long for word of the combined Maundy Thursday service to fly through the gossip channels of the congregation as the phones of parishioners rang off the hook. It would seem the prospect of the service was not as much of a slam dunk as it had first appeared.

At this point, serious behind-the-scenes strategizing among church members began. Some troubled male members from Holy Cross even met together and decided to personally visit Arnie to attempt to get him to back down from supporting the biracial service idea. So their action was a covert move designed to try to destroy the idea of a service before it came to fruition. They discussed with Arnie, whom they saw as the more moderate of the two men, the "inadvisability" of the plan, claiming the concept was "lacking in wisdom and basic common sense." But nevertheless, both Ned and Arnie remained resolute.

I truly believed in the need to take a stand on racial issues, but translating that need into reality was the courageous part, and I was anything but courageous. I appreciated the incredible message the biracial service would send to the community at large, but at what personal risk? Ned's job? His career? Our future? Who knew where this "inadvisable" idea would take us.

The entire nation was in the middle of parallel social volcanic upheavals; civil rights issues, anti-war marches, and women's equality demonstrations all took center stage in the national news. After all, Vietnam War dissenters had ultimately, on March 31, forced the president of the United States to announce he would not seek reelection for office. This was a truly stunning turn of events just six weeks before the scheduled biracial communion service. Social unrest was in the air everywhere.

For a good slice of the citizenry in the United States, the different protest movements combined into one force that appeared to stand as an evil threat to this country. Protestors were seen as disruptive malcontents—or, even worse, a conspiracy theory purported that protestors were secretly Communists committed to taking over the country. The civil rights movement, the anti-war movement, and the feminist movement were shaking up the status quo in undeniably threatening ways. And this biracial communion service between a black Lutheran church and a white Lutheran church in the Deep South played right into this troubling narrative.

Ned and I never discussed what we would do if Ned lost his job as a result of this extreme idea. I went through each day in a fog of cowardice and immaturity. My idea of what our lives would be like had already taken an unsettling turn with the realization that no one would hire me for a teaching job. Now Ned's radical civil rights commitment was beginning to leave us as potential homeless outcasts in this Southern society we had so eagerly embraced just a few short months before. Trying to talk to Ned about this was useless. He only wanted to hear about how wonderful the whole plan was, and anything else was a demonstration of my disloyalty to him.

What happened next came completely out of the blue for me. As circumstances heated up, a second voter assembly meeting was demanded by church members. This was predictable, I guess. What wasn't predictable was that many church members, after hearing of the biracial service, decided the next voter assembly meeting should be open to *all* members, women included. Now this was an incredulous demand, because within the fabric of the Lutheran Church—Missouri Synod, women were considered not equal to the task of decision-making on church matters, and thus the voter assembly was exclusively male in each congregation.

The stakes of this combined communion service twisted the congregation governance structure into an enormous power shift. How had this happened? I think it would be safe to say that stereotypes of women's roles were quietly being reexamined, thanks in great part to the powerful feminist movement. Maybe even for some church men, it would seem that the possibility of more souls boosting the cause they espoused would be a fair trade-off for opening up the male-dominated governing structure of the congregation to women—at least temporarily. But the truth was that nobody wanted to discuss this temporary loss of good male-dominated Lutheran church values, values that had always clearly excluded women. People just claimed they wanted women to be included in the second voter assembly—with no explanation.

So Ned set up a second meeting that would be open to all church members, male and female. In paraphrasing the words of Tillie, the wonderful maid from the movie, *Guess Who's Coming to Dinner,* all hell had broken loose at Holy Cross Lutheran Church in Mobile, Alabama.

CHAPTER ELEVEN

Another Vote

On the night of the second voter assembly meeting, people started filing into the church sanctuary early. Serious faces prevented easy smiles, setting a strained tone in the stuffy, humid air. Since Ned had arrived in Mobile, the struggle to see racial issues through the radical lens of the life of Jesus had been an important theme at the church. But it was no secret that some members perceived this theme as overshadowing the "legitimate" gospel. And these members believed their pastor should be solely focused on this "legitimate" gospel message, not on things like racial issues. Uncomfortable, and in some cases, downright angry, this group felt that Ned had become way out of line as the pastor of their church.

Members whom we had not seen regularly at church for quite some time began filing into the sanctuary along with loyal folks who attended each Sunday morning. The filtered light from the setting sun gave the space an almost otherworldly feel. I didn't know who'd decided to hold the meeting in the church sanctuary instead of the parish hall, but I thought the choice was a good one. This was not a night to get off track with casual, incidental stories of daily life as was usually the case in the boxy, cavernous parish hall. This was a night to grapple with the basics of how we, as a congregation of Christian believers, saw ourselves witnessing to the turbulent times in which we were living. And I believe the lovely long windows of the church sanctuary, tempered by the classic warm wooden pews, promoted deep reflection.

Connections to the soul flowed from the core of the energy, the sacred altar area. It was, after all, the profound space where babies were baptized, communion was shared, thanksgiving prayers were offered, and petitions for the suffering, and for the dead, were lifted up. Without question, the altar was the reminder of God's presence in our midst. And so it seemed the sanctuary was the appropriate location to discuss matters of this import.

By the time the meeting began, about forty-five church members had gathered. This was fewer than a normal Sunday-morning church service, but it was still a remarkable turnout for a midweek, hastily called church meeting. The group was fairly evenly divided between men and women members. Most men were dressed in the suits, white shirts, and ties they had worn to work that day, and the women wore church-appropriate dresses.

I didn't know exactly what any of the members thought about the situation, except, of course, for Billy John and Bernice. My overwhelming need for privacy in my marriage precluded the idea of having close friends in the congregation. Because of this aloofness, I guess, I was a bit like an outside observer. So I felt quite alone sitting on the aisle of one of the back rows. As far as I was concerned, my husband was our combined voice in church affairs. Besides, I wasn't technically even a member of the congregation. I often felt as though I were little more than window dressing in this church bubble, and for some reason that was OK with me, especially that night.

Sitting there alone, I realized I had arrived at a peaceful place: whatever was to be was to be. I didn't know if Ned would lose his job over his effort to unite the two churches for a biracial service. Nor did I know what a job loss would mean for us. But surprisingly, my anxiety was gone. Somehow, over the past few days, I had come to the understanding that I could accept the outcome no matter what it was. I don't know how this happened; it just had.

No one came to sit with me, but that was all right. Between the first row of pews and the altar rail, my committed husband, wearing his one-and-only suit, and a black clergy shirt with his white clerical collar, paced about slowly in nervous patterns next to William Young, the president of the congregation. Neither said a word to the other.

A tense iciness flowed through the space as William opened the meeting, asking Pastor Milner, as he referred to Ned, to give a prayer for God's guidance during the gathering. After the prayer, William made a nervously polite attempt to welcome everyone, and then he quickly jumped to the matter at hand. He asked Ned to explain his thinking behind the proposed idea of a biracial communion service. William had passed the combined church meeting issue to Ned as though it were an extremely hot potato, and it was.

Self-reliant and seemingly unconcerned, Ned stepped in front of the group and began to frame his thoughts. Wanting to defuse as much animosity as possible, he spoke in quiet, nonthreatening tones, retelling the details surrounding the anniversary service at Grace, where black Lutherans had been left out of the celebration plans altogether at first. He continued to share how he and Arnie had felt the need to denounce institutional bigotry. Then he talked of the challenge they felt to reinforce the change-of-heart message demonstrated in the more inclusive invitations from Grace.

Coming to the heart of the plan, Ned stated his belief that the proposed service might be a solid way to begin healing deep racial wounds between black and white Lutherans in Mobile. He reminded people that Jesus's commandment to "love one another" flowed from that original communion gathering on that first Maundy Thursday. Taking a deep breath, he declared, "I believe we need to make sure this message consumes our everyday living. It is about time for us, as Christians, to show the rest of the world what God's love looks like in action. This combined service should give us a wonderful opportunity to do just that."

A long silence followed. People were mulling over their responses. Then William stood up again and, with a shakiness to his voice, opened the meeting to anyone who wanted to speak. People continued to sit quietly for several more moments, though. Wondering who would be the first to break the silence, I looked over at Bernice and Billy John, who were sitting just across the aisle from me.

Bernice kept forcefully twisting her hands together until all I could see were large red knots in her lap. The muscles in her neck and face were taut. Next to her, exuding an attitude of *person in charge*, Billy John sat looking as though he had been forcibly plastered against the back of the pew, his thick arms crossed over his broad chest strong and defensively. But neither Billy John nor Bernice made a move to even stand, much less speak. They just sat there.

Finally, Norm Cormier—a new member who had recently joined the church with his wife and family because they liked Ned's sermons—stood up and spoke. His rather quiet Northern voice stated without hesitation that he agreed with the rationale Ned gave for the joint service. He said he felt it might be a small but important start to heal relationships with black people in general, and black Lutherans in particular. Then he sat down. Another silence followed for several moments. Perhaps the sacredness of the space where we all worshiped each Sunday tempered angry outbursts a bit. But maybe that was just naive thinking on my part.

Two more men then, to my surprise, stood in turn to make comments thoughtfully defending the biracial communion service idea as well. People were reaching deep inside, weighing personal feelings on this matter against what had just been shared by others, and the unsettled energy was palpable. Was this what grace, mysteriously at work, looked like? I really didn't know the answer, but it somehow seemed like a sound hypothesis.

Then out of nowhere, Harriet Miers slowly got to her feet. Harriet was the unmarried middle-aged daughter of an elderly shut-in couple. Because of poor health, her parents never attended church anymore. The Mierses clearly did still see themselves as devout members of the church, nonetheless, and Ned, as part of his pastoral duties, took communion to them at home each week. While living with her parents, Harriet attended church services regularly every Sunday. She was their designated connection to the lifeblood of the congregation, and she volunteered in many ways, most importantly as a member of the altar guild.

Setting her solid, matronly black shoes squarely on the floor, and with her hands on the pew in front of her, her face in its customary dour expression, she pulled herself slowly to her feet. Her simple flowered housedress and baggy sweater hung loose on her boney frame. Positioned in the light of a close window near the front of the room, Harriet seemed to understand the gravity of being the first woman ever to speak at a voter assembly meeting in this congregation.

She softly grappled for words. "I don't think . . ." And then she paused. "I don't think . . . ah . . . maybe I can't . . . ah . . . take communion." Her face was turning blotchy red, and then after another long pause, she pulled her knit sweater close around her thin waist. Harriet slowly finished with, "When we take communion here, we all drink from the same chalice. Could we . . . maybe . . . take communion from small individual cups on the Maundy Thursday service—small individual cups like pastor uses when he gives my folks communion at home?"

The controversial idea of sharing the same communion cup with the invited black guests at the biracial service had finally been verbalized. It came as no surprise that the basic notion of the combined service itself, where people would be expected to sit next to invited black guests, wasn't as objectionable as the idea of everyone drinking communion wine out of the same vessel. A good bit of whispering among attendees followed Harriet's comments. This portion of the biracial service plan was causing people to talk—if not to the group as a whole, at least to one another. Harriet had politely opened the discussion to what would prove to be the gist of the antagonism.

Finally, Louie Ittmann, a staunch church volunteer and a dear friend to most people in the room, stood up. In his wonderfully melodic New Orleans accent and with his usual impish grin, he began to tell the story of his time on board a US battleship as a Marine in World War II, the night before the horrific battle of Okinawa. In typical Louie fashion, he threw his head back a little and widened his smile as he continued telling his story. In the dark of that fearful night, Louie recalled how he'd heard the announcement belowdecks that anyone wanting to receive communion should join the chaplain up on deck. Louie said that just about every soldier on board that ship, Native Americans, African Americans, Hispanic Americans, all Americans alike, quickly gathered up on deck.

Louie was clear in detailing how the chaplain's invitation to take part was inclusive. There were no belief requirements, no racial requirements, no gender or sexual orientation requirements to meet—there were absolutely no stipulations whatsoever. All that was needed was a desire to take part in the sacrament.

Louie talked about how the chaplain had seemed puzzled for a moment when it came time to distribute the wine after the bread had been passed to each man. Then the chaplain had asked the Marine standing next to him for his helmet. The chaplain had poured the communion wine into the man's helmet, and the helmet was passed around. Everyone—short, tall, black, brown, white, thin, heavy, courageous, fearful—took a small sip from the same helmet and then carefully passed it on to the next person. No one gave one moment of thought to the helmet they were drinking from, or to whomever was standing next to them.

The story hit its target full bore as Louie stated, "It was the most memorable communion experience of my life." Louie's easy smile defused the disquiet when he finished with a soft chuckle, saying, "I don't see how it much matters some twenty-plus years later if we use a common communion cup or a war helmet to serve communion wine to our guests here in our church. Communion wine is God's gift to us. Why we are getting bogged down on the details of how it gets distributed is beyond me." Silence filled with a sense of relief rolled through the room as Louie sat down.

Finally, President Young broke the quiet and thanked Louie for his words. He once again asked for any other comments, looking around at the faces in front of him. It took time for all of us to process Louie's contribution. Then Roy Morgan, an old, perpetual grump, stood up. In a voice filled with disdain, Roy said he thought we still should look into individual cups anyway, finishing with: "Thank you very much, Mr. Louie Ittmann." And then Roy sat down. And with those words, the grace that had flowed from Louie's healing balm had been effectively sucked out of the air.

President Young asked for other comments or questions and waited patiently for a good long time. No one said anything else— no one. The Skrimses just continued to sit, staunchly radiating unhappiness. Why they were unwilling to say anything, I really don't know. But they kept quiet.

What I do know is that when it was time for the hand vote to decide whether to go ahead with the biracial communion service, there were about twenty yes votes and about ten no votes. The combined service was approved. The remainder of the attendees never voted either way, including Billy John and Bernice.

Most of the women present, including myself, were confused as to whether we even had a vote. We didn't know if we had just been included in this special one-off meeting for the purpose of speaking our minds, or if men were serious about allowing us to become equal participants in church governance matters. But building inclusiveness of women into church decision-making would require a great deal more work in the future. On that night, everyone's energy was dedicated to other matters. Women's issues, as usual, would just have to wait.

At the end of the meeting, Ned stated, "With all due respect to our dear friend and honored veteran, Louie, we should decide whether or not to use individual cups at a future voter assembly meeting." People seemed fine with the suggestion. The extraordinary tension had dissipated, and the majority of the attendees left with feelings of warmth and friendliness. But the Skrimses, and two or three other families, radiated hostility as they left the church. Openly angry, they just marched quickly to their respective cars and then sullenly drove away.

At the next voter assembly meeting a day or two later—this time without women members—the group voted to buy and use individual cups to serve communion wine at the Maundy Thursday biracial service. And so a compromise had been worked out.

At that same meeting, after the voting and other business was completed, President Young redirected the focus. Young claimed he needed to publicly discuss a compelling issue with Ned. In a nervous voice, salted with acrimony, Young summed up the matter by stating, "Pastor Milner, as president of this congregation, I am bringing a suggestion, or even better, a request, on behalf of many congregation members. Several of us feel it would be nice if you could find your way clear to preach a sermon or two on the gospel for a change." With that, he collected his things and left the church. The shiny Maundy Thursday service victory was quickly beginning to tarnish.

Additional fallout from the second vote hit the proverbial fan the following Sunday morning. Ned stood at the door of the church as people were leaving when Billy John, with Bernice at his side, stepped up and announced loudly for all to hear, "Pastor Milner, this is our last time coming to this church. We will be finding another place to worship." Two other prominent families gave the same angry announcement as they left the church that morning.

Although it should have come as no surprise, Ned's spirits were seriously deflated by this. A significant group of hardworking, committed church members were now gone from the congregation. This included the family whose deep pockets had often held the congregation together financially.

A side of Ned felt like he had really screwed things up. After all, this was his first parish assignment right out of seminary. What was this going to look like on his resume? The thought of submitting his resignation had occurred to him, so he turned his thoughts to church hierarchy. He wondered why the upper-echelon church synod leaders hadn't come to Mobile to bail him out of this mess. Surely, they knew what was going on. He thought they could reassign him to another church position somewhere else. Retreating to a delusional victim place, Ned would privately proclaim to me, "All I wanted was to be assigned to an inner-city church after seminary. This mess at Holy Cross would never have happened if I had been sent to an inner-city church."

He deeply believed that he was responsible for destroying Holy Cross Lutheran Church, which left him with enormous guilt. And a dark night of the soul followed. But he never, and I mean never, asked me for any guidance or even saw me as having a part in any of this growing drama. I had to keep reminding myself that I was just along for the ride; it was like being an incidental spectator at a boxing match with my husband as a main contender.

Anyway, since Ned never wanted my unflinching take on anything, I kept my thoughts to myself. At least my efforts maintained a modicum of peace in the house. I tried to keep our spirits up by praising his courage and encouraging his great sense of commitment to social justice. I pretty much saw myself as his main cheerleader, whether I wanted to be or not. Wasn't that what I was supposed to do, after all? Wasn't that the role I had signed up for? I sure thought so. I was twenty-five years old, and in my insensitive, flawed way, I was all about doing what I believed was expected of me as a good wife. But as more ominous developments continued to enter our lives, even my second-rate cheerleading wouldn't be able to carry the day for us.

CHAPTER TWELVE

Martin Luther King Jr. Assassination

Seven days before the combined communion service, I made up my mind to try a recipe for jambalaya. Ned and I loved the delicious array of fresh seafood available in Mobile, and jambalaya had soon become one of our favorite dishes.

I had left the fish stew mixture on low heat all day and arrived home from work certain my attempt was going to be wonderful. I discovered my hopefulness was misplaced, though, when I served up the concoction that evening. I didn't know what I had done wrong. Maybe some of the ingredients were not as fresh as one would hope, but my effort at what was, for me, an exotic dish turned out to be really disappointing—slightly akin to seafood garbage. And after valiantly trying to eat it, Ned and I decided to just stick with a restaurant version.

We sat at our official kitchen table, a folding card table, picking at the previous night's leftovers in an effort to supplement our disastrous main dish. It was fun laughing together about the dinner catastrophe, but then the phone rang. Ned reached over to pick up the receiver on the wall. I watched, stupefied, as his face drained of color while he listened to the voice on the other end of the line. When the conversation finished, he hung up, and I saw my usually strong and confident husband sitting across from me slumped in a state of shock. He told me in deliberate, slow words that it was Jerry Pogue, a friend from the Neighborhood Organized Workers (NOW), a civil rights group. Jerry had just heard on the radio that Martin Luther King Jr. had been shot in Memphis, and that King had died from the gunshot wound. The news was truly horrifying. We both sat frozen in dazed disbelief.

Finally, after several silent moments, Ned stood up and told me the Neighborhood Organized Workers group was calling an emergency meeting right away, and he would be leaving to go. NOW members felt prompted to get together to share their profound grief over King's death and to talk about how to publicly respond as activists to the shocking news.

In the early morning hours, Ned finally returned home. I had gone to bed but wasn't asleep when he came into the room. The atmosphere of our small bedroom was filled with a sickening sadness. In quiet words, my husband related to me what had happened at the NOW meeting. He told me the conversation had focused on how to honor the memory of Dr. King. After hours of talk, the group had decided the best idea would be to organize a memorial march. King's courageous legacy had been emboldened by high-profile, peaceful civil rights marches, so this seemed the most appropriate way to pay tribute to this iconic man in his death. The group agreed on a plan for a MLK memorial march through the black communities of Mobile, scheduled for two days later.

At this meeting, Jerry, Arnie, and Ned had volunteered to help cover publicity for the march. As part of this task, the three men had left the meeting around ten o'clock and gone to Arnie's church, Faith Lutheran. They'd hunkered down in the church office and put together a flyer detailing information on the MLK march. Finally the job of mimeographing the flyers was finished. That left only distributing them to the communities and neighborhoods of Mobile county. Ned was up early the next morning to deliver flyers to outlying areas of the county with Jerry as his knowledgeable navigator. Arnie had the job of getting flyers to critical spots throughout the city and especially to the black community.

For a long time, white politicians in Mobile had diligently tried to portray the city as a genteel place where racial problems really didn't exist as in other Southern areas. Created predominantly by the white power structure, this myth denied deep, underlying fissures in race relations in Mobile and its environs.

In charge at this moment in history was this same racially tone-deaf white power structure. NOW was required to petition these city fathers the next day for a permit for the peaceful memorial march. As a demonstration of how racially out of touch the power structure really was, the city flatly denied NOW's request. Instead, these city fathers instituted an indefinite curfew. Adding insult to injury, the curfew pinpointed only black neighborhoods in Mobile.

Reeling from these high-handed city actions, NOW met to decide where to go from there. As far as the activists were concerned, the city of Mobile had treated the request for a permit to march with outright contempt. And NOW members believed that it was an inherent right to be able to peacefully march. So with the shadow of Martin Luther King Jr.'s bold life as an activist leader prominent in their decision, the group went ahead with plans for a MLK memorial march for Saturday April 6 anyway.

Enormous tension spilled over everywhere in the nation as responses to King's assassination not only brought overwhelming sadness and grief but hostility and fury in the form of racial riots in many cities. Forces opposed to these horrified and angry feelings were politically committed to holding the line no matter how much violence it would require. And as NOW saw it, here in Mobile, the city leaders had no interest in trying to find peaceful ways to bring about reconciliation, only an all-out effort to maintain what was determined to be the status quo while trampling basic civil rights.

Waking up before the alarm that Saturday morning, I was extremely unsettled looking at the beginning rays of light poring through the crack between the curtains. My brain was wallowing in the memories of former civil rights marches, especially the one from Selma to Montgomery. Reminiscences of the horrible violence perpetrated against the activists sent shivers down my spine as I thought about the water hoses, dogs, and clubs that had been used against the march's nonviolent participants. I didn't have any idea how to prepare emotionally for the possibility of violence. And, in cowardice, I kept wondering if I should even go to the march in the first place. This was, if the truth be told, Ned's heroic life mission, not mine.

My husband was lost in the righteous drama of it all. As he lay asleep in bed next to me, I thought of him as always being too busy taking care of earth-shattering matters to care enough to talk me through my fear. He didn't seem to even consider me a part of his "momentous" work in the first place. I saw myself as wallpaper in his life, left completely alone to find my own way through everything.

What a pathetically lonely and anxious little Northern transplant I was. I struggled with these insidious thoughts for a long time. Then climbing out of bed that morning, I stood looking in the mirror and saw a scared little familiar face looking back. Something in my brain clicked as I took stock of that face. I knew, somehow, that I needed to get control of my angst. I knew I had to make up my mind to do the right thing, come hell or high water. And so, right then and there, I came to the certainty that I was going to march, and that was that.

Ned awakened and quickly rolled out of bed. He dressed in dark slacks with his black shirt and white clerical collar while I pulled on a sleeveless cotton dress and flat-heeled comfortable shoes. We each quickly drank a cup of coffee and swallowed down a piece of toast. Our plan was to be out the door by eight o'clock. We were ahead of schedule as we popped into the car and started off toward Davis Street, the cultural center of the black community in Mobile, and the starting place of the march. We spent the short trip almost in silence, no discussion of what-ifs, just the basics on how to get where we were going. The time for personal discussion of any problems we might encounter had passed. It seemed time now to focus on doing what we believed we needed to do.

After parking some blocks away, we walked directly to the starting point. Looking around at the street, it was clear a great deal of preplanning had occurred on the part of the city of Mobile, and the state of Alabama. Lining each side of Davis Street in both directions and facing the street were Alabama state troopers. They stood about fifteen to twenty feet apart holding rifles upright in front of them with fixed bayonets, clubs hanging from their belts. Dressed in full combat gear, the troopers exuded an incredibly menacing presence.

Stepping cautiously between state troopers into the line of march on Davis Street, we met up with Judy and Arnie. Soon we saw the Cormier family from our church. Ned had called some church members he thought might be interested in attending the planned march, and so Norm and his wife, Amarant, had showed up. This family had explained the meaning of the march, along with the possibility of violence, to their three young sons. Then they'd given each of the boys the nonjudgmental, free choice to come along or stay home. The youngest, eleven-year-old Thomas, had decided to join his parents in the march. So with the three Cormiers standing nearby, Arnie, Judy, Ned, and I lined up in about the second or third row from the front of the march. I was almost at the very end of the row, close to the side of the street. As people began to line up, very little was said. But there was an undeniable determination in the looks that were exchanged.

At the front of the march, Jerry Pogue proudly stood holding a huge flagpole with the American flag waving boldly. Next to him our friend James Dixon carried the Christian flag on another over-sized flagpole. There was no music, no ringleader with a bullhorn, just large groups of people—black marchers mostly, but certainly some whites like our small group—who fell into a silent, dignified mass lined up side by side in rows stretching several blocks. Later reports claimed as many as several thousand people had showed up, but I can't testify to that. All I know is more marchers were there than I had ever anticipated. The strongest memory of that moment for me was of an almost boundless space filled with an extraordinarily purposeful energy.

At last, as the mass of people slowly started to move forward, my heart began beating with an intensity I had never before experienced; I thought it would jump right out of my chest. I found my hands shaking uncontrollably at my sides, but all I could do was continue to put one foot in front of the other.

Keeping my head down made me feel safer in some weird way, so my next vivid memory was of looking over to the side of the street where my eyes became slowly mesmerized by the heavy combat boots every fifteen feet or so, each pair pointing in my direction. The boots were, of course, on the feet of Alabama state troopers, and these crusty, colossal symbols of power began hypnotizing me as we walked along. The only sound I could hear was the muffled thuds of hundreds and hundreds of feet clad in regular street shoes striking the pavement as my brain was caught up in the passing boots.

There was a strange sensation in the air. A bold energy was in fact wildly bouncing about in the humid atmosphere, and I soon recognized the feel of what had to be raw courage. It miraculously flowed like a cool steam from one marcher to the next, floating mysteriously in the warm sea breeze. The contagious force slowly filled my lungs, releasing apprehension and giving strength to my legs. As the energy worked its magic through my system, I found myself slowly straightening my neck and holding my head a bit higher, focusing on the scene in front of me, rather than on the combat boots.

Then somewhere behind us on the march route, someone began singing. Out of the courage-saturated air, the song "We

Shall Overcome" made its way down the lines of marchers until a sea of voices joined in. From out of nowhere, a sense of peace permeated deep inside my psyche. With great certainty, I finally felt like I was just where I was supposed to be, doing what I believed to be right. It was a memorable moment, indeed.

Thankfully, the peaceful march ended with no incidents of violence, despite the fact that no permit had been issued. But the NOW organization had sent a message to the white power structure of Mobile that not everything was fine within the racial fabric of the city. Hundreds of caring citizens of the city of Mobile had courageously demonstrated a commitment to the civil rights movement in this march memorializing the life of Dr. Martin Luther King Jr. And for that we were extraordinarily grateful.

But deep anger was still evident over the death of King, sharply defining the message that things needed to change in Mobile race relations on fundamental levels like education, employment, and voter registration. The good news was that a surprising number of Mobile residents seemed committed to seeing these changes start to happen, if the large numbers at the unpermitted march was any indication.

King's assassination, like the scene on Billy John's boat dock, had given Ned an uncompromising obsession with civil rights causes. Up to that point in his life, Ned had tried to balance his obligations to pastor the Holy Cross congregation with his increasing need to work on behalf of peace and justice issues. That effort had become very precarious. After the hateful words Billy John had spewed out on his boat dock, and now with the incredible loss of Dr. King, Ned knew his priorities were moving into unexplored places. He wasn't sure what that was going to mean for his job as pastor, but he knew he had to increase his commitment to civil rights issues.

CHAPTER THIRTEEN

Maundy Thursday Service

Exactly one week after the assignation of Dr. Martin Luther King Jr., members from two Lutheran congregations in the Deep South—one entirely black, and one entirely white—gathered together on that Maundy Thursday to worship and commune as one body—a truly remarkable occurrence. I would like to think the event would have pleased Dr. King in some small way.

Up to the day before the service, a city-instituted curfew in black neighborhoods was still in effect. The curfew acted as a lid on activities in black neighborhoods. Concern over potential behavior that might turn riotous even caused a few black leaders to patrol in their own neighborhoods with loaded shotguns, especially in front of gun shops, to keep people from breaking in and arming themselves. Anger over King's assassination—especially in the black community—was bone deep.

Early in the week, Arnie met with the Mobile chief of police to find out when the curfew would be lifted. If the curfew were to continue, it would shut down plans for the combined service, as no one from the Faith Lutheran congregation could go to the joint service without fear of arrest. Even after Arnie explained all this, the Mobile police chief was indifferent, offering no helpful answers.

Finally, on the morning of Maundy Thursday, city authorities lifted the curfew. Arnie phoned leaders of his congregation with the good news, but there was without question still a good deal of trepidation over the tense situation. So after much discussion, courageous members of Faith Lutheran decided to try to cover each other's backs as much as possible and carpool together to the service. The plan was to caravan with Arnie to Holy Cross to try to minimize the chance of any unintended racial incidents, like being stopped—illegally—for driving in white communities. They were committed to this historic act of worshiping together, even though just getting to the church itself was a demonstration of great bravery.

Earlier in the day, a drowning rain had swept up from the bay as if there had been an effort to wash the air of tense, unsettled feelings. Thankfully, the weather cleared by six o'clock in the evening, and the last piece of the biracial church service drama was ready to unfold.

I was at the church early with Ned, as he needed time to set things up for the communion part of the service. Witnessing my determined husband, a little agitated and displaying a level of anxiety I hadn't seen in him before, pulled me deeper into his world. At about seven o'clock, I took a seat on a pew toward the front of the almost-empty church. Knowing I couldn't change the direction of how things were going in my life, short of leaving Ned, I relaxed a little and hoped for the best possible outcome for the evening. Leaving my husband was not an option I would consider.

By seven thirty, the church had filled with about seventy-five people, about one-third coming from Arnie's church. The seductive fragrance of night-blooming jasmine floated lazily about in the heavy humidity. As it turned out, there was no "white section" or "black section" in the church. People just seemed to easily sit with each other, which was a sight to behold in and of itself. Watching hosts and guests talk warmly before the service was amazing. My psyche was touched by the sight of this biracial group actually making extraordinary efforts to worship together in this place—it had truly happened.

Ned began with the age-old liturgy of the Maundy Thursday service. The invaluable spiritual scaffolding begins with, "The Lord be with you," and the congregation responds, "And also with you." As the litany progressed, prayers showered over us with an intensity that could only have been God's love at work. A lovely sense of unity started to expand as we sang the familiar hymns, "Rock of Ages" and "Were You There." It was all coming together as if it was meant to be.

Arnie had agreed to preach the sermon, and then, at the last minute, he and Ned decided on a dialogue sermon between the two of them. The idea worked well as each became more thoughtfully in the moment by responding to the comments of the other.

Then the time for the communion portion of the service came. It was stunningly beautiful as racially mixed groups of about fifteen or so walked up the aisle, knelt down together at the altar rail, and solemnly joined each other in the sharing of the bread and wine.

A wonderful feeling had filled the sanctuary—a feeling of wholeness that was hard to describe. And I could only hope a tiny shred of healing between these two groups of God's beloved children might have begun that night. From the conversations after the service between Faith members and Holy Cross members, it seemed like people felt comforted by what had just happened. And to me, that in itself was a positive victory, especially in the shadow of the life and death of Dr. Martin Luther King Jr.

And on this same day in history, the Civil Rights Act of 1968 was signed by President Johnson, just as though the *Good Housekeeping* stamp of approval had been put on the joint communion service between these two brave, forward-looking churches in the Deep South.

This remarkable act, of course, made it a federal crime to "by force or by threat of force, injure, intimidate, or interfere with anyone . . . by reason of their race, color, religion, or national origin," a major milestone in race relations legislation in the United States.

CHAPTER FOURTEEN

Tired of
Being White

The welfare office where I worked was a rambling old one-story structure built in the early 1900s as the county hospital. It had been converted to office space sometime back, but a rather grand stone front porch still covered the entrance wall. I often thought maybe a hospital such as this might have accommodated poor Zelda Fitzgerald, wife of F. Scott Fitzgerald, when she had been hospitalized for mental problems in the South, and so I frequently referred to my office as "Zelda's Place." Although the building was now quite shabby in appearance, it clearly had an old, Deep South architectural appeal, and it sat on a large, uncluttered slice of land.

It was midafternoon on Wednesday, June 12, 1968, just ten weeks after Dr. Martin Luther King Jr. had been assassinated, and less than one week after the assassination of Senator Bobby Kennedy, brother of President John Fitzgerald Kennedy. Electrically charged racial tensions consumed every hollow space of life everywhere.

Sitting in Zelda's Place off the main hall, wearing a new sleeveless white eyelet dress, I was busy with paperwork, which always seemed to need attention. Then one of the secretaries came in and told me some man was outside on the porch wanting to talk to me about something important. Brushing my short hair back, I walked out of my office, into the hall, around the collection of secretarial desks, and onto the large front porch. To my surprise, standing there in front of me was my good friend Arnie.

I was startled with Arnie's odd appearance, though. He stood there methodically shifting his lanky frame back and forth from one long leg to the other, his facial muscles uncomfortably strained. Asking what had brought him to my office in the middle of the afternoon, he touched my arm and told me maybe I should sit down on the stone ledge behind me.

I began growing a little anxious. As I dropped onto the cool stone, Arnie said in very measured words, "Molly, Ned has been arrested and is in jail in Prichard. He was arrested with about a hundred black people during a march this afternoon." In a stupor, I just stared into Arnie's honest blue eyes, not comprehending his words very quickly. Then, after a long pause, he continued. "Ned was the only white person arrested in the group of marchers." My hands, folded in my lap, felt numb as trickles of perspiration started to run down the back of my neck. Then Arnie said, "I think you should come with me to the jail to see what we can do." He finished with some anguish, saying, "Molly, it should have been me that was arrested."

It took a bit of time for me to really hear his words. I gazed out to the parking area, looking at nothing in particular. Thoughts exploded in my brain: How could this be, Ned arrested and in jail? He had never said a word about a march to me. How had this happened? How could he treat me with such disdain by not even mentioning his plans to me? Was he all right? What was I supposed to do about it? I felt utterly helplessness.

In a state of complete shock, I stood up slowly, nervously straightening my dress. Walking directly to my supervisor's office,

I knocked on the door. John Hill had been sympathetic to civil rights causes all along, so I had no hesitation telling him the situation. I asked John if I could leave for the rest of the day, and he said of course.

In my little blue car, I carefully followed Arnie in his VW Bug to Prichard. We pulled into spaces in the busy parking area close to the old, run-down complex of city offices, which included the jail building. I recognized several faces from different civil rights meetings as I tried to take in the crowd of agitated people milling around. Arnie shepherded me over to a serious-looking, middle-aged man dressed in a dark suit, a white shirt, and a tie, with large, heavy glasses. I remembered speaking with this man, Dave Brock, at one of the recent movement gatherings at Spring Hill College. Dave was an activist working for American Friends Service Committee, an organization that had been providing support to civil rights causes in Mobile for some time.

Dave took my arm and led me over to a less-crowded area. He said he had just found out some important information: Ned had been incarcerated in the black side of the segregated jail. This surprising decision made by the Prichard police relieved a huge fear shared by many of the activists, as they felt this would actually be the safest place for Ned.

Then Dave took me over to the jail-building wall where I saw a long, narrow window. Heavy bars secured the little opening, but with help of some people yelling into the window, I soon saw Ned's face through the bars. I couldn't believe my eyes, though, because he was grinning back at me as if he were having a perfectly fine old time.

The experience was surreal, indeed. After swallowing hard, I realized how grateful I was that he was OK, but I could make no sense of his strange, almost celebratory behavior. It was comforting for me to see his smile and hear him say in his own voice that he was all right. But I really couldn't join in on this rather heady sense of excitement. My mind was swirling in a cauldron of shock and fear, and my escalating anger made it hard to say anything to him aside from "I love you." With what felt to me like very little sensitivity and a great deal of showmanship for the people in the vicinity, Ned returned the same words to me, a big grin still plastered across his face.

So my husband was in jail. Walking away from the window, I thought the situation couldn't get any worse, but I was wrong. Dave took my arm again and steered me over to a shady spot. In a rather quiet voice, he added another twist to the already daunting narrative. Dave told me that, as the police were forcibly shoving Ned into the paddy wagon, a journalist had asked Ned if he had anything to say about what was happening. My husband had audaciously responded to the journalist with the words: "I'm sick of being white." Well, there it was, the cherry on the arrest cake. It was not enough for me to have to grapple with the fact that my husband had been the only white face in the group of over one hundred folks arrested, but he had also bombastically thrown words out into the wind that were sure to antagonize a whole lot more people than those who were already seething over his behavior.

I struggled to collect my thoughts as I stood there in the parking lot of the Prichard jail, but it was almost more than I could manage. Arnie and Dave talked further, and I stepped back for a while, trying to figure out what was happening. Arnie seemed to understand I was a bit overwhelmed. He told me I should probably go home, gather up a few things, get the dog, and then come to their house. The suggestion sounded perfect to me because I couldn't think of a single thing to do next on my own. I was grateful for Arnie.

The overpowering stench of sulfur dioxide from the paper mills hung especially heavy in the air that late afternoon, adding insult to injury. To describe my state of mind as shell-shocked would be an understatement. I got to my car and dropped into the seat; my mind was reeling. I knew I would need bail money to get Ned out, but I had no idea how to raise it. We owned no property, or anything of value that could be put up as collateral. I felt utterly alone, confused, and terrified. So in a Scarlett O'Hara–type response, I finally decided I would just think about all this crazy stuff later, and I started the car and drove the few miles through Mobile to my house on Merritt Drive.

As I unlocked the back door and walked into the kitchen, the phone rang. I caught it on the third ring. An unknown male voice steeped in a deep Southern drawl came on the line with words that shot through my brain like lightning, "Mrs. Milner—this is the Mobile Police Department. We're just calling you to tell you not to bother to call us tonight because we won't be responding to any request for help from you. You and your husband deserve whatever happens to you, and we don't think any of us should have to bother to help protect you." Then click—the line went dead.

I stood frozen in stunned disbelief. Hanging up the receiver with an uncontrollably shaking hand, I really didn't know how to process what I had just heard. My thoughts swirled wildly. Surely I had misunderstood the terse message. What had he said again? Was this some kind of joke?

Standing in the kitchen, almost paralyzed with fear, I heard the phone ring again. On the second ring, I picked up the receiver, thinking it was the police, this time wanting to tell me they had made a mistake. Of course they would be there for us—but no such luck.

This time, it was another unknown male with a particularly raspy voice and an unusually heavy Southern country accent. Slowly drawing each syllable out, he said, "Mrs. Mil-lin-er, we-all don't like your hus-band very much, and we want to take care of him—reeeal good. We know where y'all live and where that church is that he works at . . . And when we find him . . . and we sure will, we're gunna pour gas-o-line on him and set him on fire . . . and we hope y'all are there to watch." The voice then laughed raucously, and the line clicked off.

Alone in the semidarkness of twilight with my hand still clutching the receiver, I felt as though I were a solid stone statue frozen to my kitchen floor. I couldn't move. Then my incredible dog, Tallulah, lovingly nuzzled my hand, bringing me back to the present. My one true connection to reality was the thought: *Tallulah is here. I am not alone.*

As quickly as I could, I gathered up a few pieces of clothing, my toothbrush, and Tallulah's leash, and then I sprinted out the back door. I ran to the carport, and after popping Tallulah into the back seat, I jumped into the car.

As I drove off to Arnie and Judy's place, it seemed like I was in the middle of a nightmare. My thoughts spun out of control in my brain. Surely this wasn't happening to me. Whatever had Ned been thinking to put me in such danger? How could he have been so completely thoughtless? Why hadn't he at least told me about the march the night before? How long had he been thinking about getting arrested? Why had I never considered that anything like this might happen?

As the questions thrashed around in my head, my anger toward Ned grew exponentially. I knew he saw his actions as something that shouldn't be questioned. He believed his decisions were simply a part of his calling as a follower of Jesus. So any concern for me shouldn't have any place on his agenda. That was his mantra, after all.

But, my God, he wasn't alone in the consequences of his behavior. How did it happen that he was the only white man arrested with one hundred black people? Why did he decide to stay in the march after marchers were told by police they would be arrested if they did not step out onto the curb? Clearly his white activist friends had made the decision to leave the line of march. Why, oh why, was he such a damned in-your-face radical?

I pulled into a parking space at Judy and Arnie's vintage World War II brick apartment complex and leaped out of the car, keeping Tallulah close to me on a short leash. Racing to the door, I pounded loudly, hardly able to wait for it to open. Finally, stepping inside, I felt I could at last take a breath. Collapsing into a chair, I slowly told Judy and Arnie about the threatening phone calls. They sat staring at me in silence for several moments. Then Judy said she wanted me to stay there with them that night, and for as long as it would take to feel safe again. I was so intensely grateful for these courageous friends.

After a bit, Arnie said we should probably go back to Prichard to check on the bail process. Even though I knew he was right, it was difficult for me to get myself out of the chair and to the door.

The next thing I knew, I was standing in front of an old, beat-up desk in the front room of the Prichard jail. The air was filled with foul smells and traces of Mace as people crowded in little groups around the confined space. I looked into the rather languid eyes of a large middle-aged man dressed in an ill-fitting, cheesy-looking police uniform who was sitting behind the desk. His police cap was pulled low over his forehead, and he spoke in slow, sluggish tones. I asked him about the legal status of my husband. He answered, "Yeah, little lady, we got that man, George Mil—Mil-lin-ner, in custody here, and you oughta be glad he's in with 'his own kind,' at least for now. No bail has been set for his release yet, though. That's all I'm gunna tell ya." A smirky smile began to pull at the corners of his mouth as he waved Arnie and me back away from the desk. Then Arnie went over to talk with some men I didn't recognize, and I went back outside.

In the dark parking area, Judy and I were part of the group of friends and family of the incarcerated marchers milling about trying to figure out what was going to happen next. Then out of nowhere, we heard loud voices begin to yell at us: "Disperse!" The police were apparently becoming panicked over the crowd of concerned people gathered outside the jail. The next thing we knew, police in riot gear and helmets came charging out of the police station with guns pointed at us, demanding again: "Disperse!" In fear, Judy and I scurried off to the car, climbing inside for safety.

After a while, Dave Brock and Arnie came to the car with some welcome news. They told us that after a lot of negotiation and arm-twisting, some black businessmen and homeowners had stepped up and put their homes on the line as collateral for bail for everyone arrested. Ned's bail was included in this generous act. So I never even knew how much his bail was.

This was a seminal moment for Ned and me, though. As I look back on what followed, I realize that this was just the first step in our adjunct membership to the hugely complex and enormously generous African American world of the Deep South. Pretty much everything safe and good that happened to us from then on, until we moved back to Ohio over a year later, was because of our new status as honorary members of the black community. As the years pass, the overwhelming generosity of this gift grows even more precious in my memory.

Although my husband had chosen to be arrested and to make a public statement that shocked the sensibilities of most people in the white community, his behavior did cause an immense closing of the ranks around him in the large black community, cementing the bond they felt for the only white man volunteering to stand with them in a time of defining crises.

Later that evening, after being released on bail, the marchers gathered in the church where the march had been organized. The courageous people who had put their houses up as collateral were introduced, and an attorney for the NAACP talked about what should be coming next within the legal system. Soon the arrested marchers would have to appear in court for a hearing, and possible sentencing. After the meeting, Arnie and Ned finally came back to the apartment where Judy and I were waiting.

Seeing Ned for the first time after his release stirred up a mixed bag of feelings for me. I was so glad he was safe and unharmed, and I hugged him close. Yet I was also extraordinarily angry because I thought that his behavior had put both of us in great physical danger. What was almost a greater injustice to me was that I hadn't even been given a warning of what he had planned to do before he did it, as though his actions had no bearing on my life whatsoever. I couldn't help but feel completely betrayed.

But as was usual in our relationship, for the most part, I buried the anger. It seemed so self-absorbed compared to the remarkably heroic action that Ned had apparently taken. His dramatic arrest had already inflamed strong feelings far and wide, and my anger wasn't going to change what had happened. Deep down, I was ashamed I couldn't be more proud of his very courageous act of civil disobedience. So Judy and I sat quietly and listened to Ned and Arnie's recounting of the Prichard job march.

City government in Prichard—a small, mostly black, very poor town that shares a border with the north side of the city of Mobile—was entirely white. Job opportunities available for black residents were nonexistent beyond janitors, house cleaners, and childcare workers. Reverend Arthur Ray, pastor of a large black church in Prichard, and other leaders, had asked civil rights organizations in the Mobile area to support them in a march to protest lack of job opportunities in their city government. So the Prichard job march had been organized for Wednesday, June 12.

Leaders had obtained a permit weeks in advance, and appropriate city officials had signed off. The march was scheduled to start in front of Reverend Ray's church early in the afternoon, and over a hundred marchers gathered. Jerry Pogue positioned himself at the front proudly hoisting a large American flag on a substantial flagpole.

Just a few minutes before the starting time of the march, a Prichard city official, along with the police chief, purposefully walked up to people standing at the front of the gathered marchers and announced that the permit to march had just been withdrawn and that the group would have to disperse. News that the permit had been withdrawn quickly flowed back through the huge group of folks waiting to start. What followed was a great deal of confusion and angry responses. After a few moments, the consensus of the group was clear: *Let's go ahead and march anyway.*

So, in unity, the marchers organized and started to walk down the street with renewed determination. Singing "We Shall Overcome," this group of brave folks nonviolently walked to the end of the first block, where Alabama state troopers stood blocking the street. Wearing riot gear, they stood shoulder to shoulder with guns pointed straight at the marchers. At this obstacle, leaders at the front of the march made an unexpected right turn onto a side street, leaving the state troopers looking a bit embarrassed and chagrined.

Tension intensified under the hot, humid afternoon sun, and the noise level increased as the marchers continued slowly along their new route. In a state of confusion, police and state troopers broke rank after the marchers had—all of a sudden—turned onto another street. They ran helter-skelter along the sidewalks of the second block in order to regroup at the end of that block for another attempt to stop the forward progress of the group. At the end of the second block, state troopers and Prichard police quickly formed another human wall by again standing shoulder to shoulder with their guns pointing at the marchers.

The police didn't seem to have a well-thought-out plan. Additionally, it was clear the police hadn't anticipated such a large group of marchers. At the end of the second block, the police pulled out bullhorns, and the amplified message left no doubt in people's minds: The march was illegal. Everyone must either step out of the line of march and onto the curb, or be arrested.

Waiting only a few brief seconds for participants to decide what to do, police started to make their move. The majority of marchers defiantly stood their ground, while others simply sat down peacefully where they were in the middle of the street. Then these courageous folks began to be dragged roughly one by one to waiting police vehicles. It was hardly a battle of equals, Alabama state troopers in their black uniforms with helmets, boots, riot gear, guns, and bayonets pitted against common, peaceful everyday citizens dressed in normal daytime clothes and shoes with nothing in their hands but signs protesting unequal employment opportunities. But then, nothing about the day was equal or fair.

Jerry Pogue, with his large American flag, and James Dixon, who had been carrying the Christian flag, were among the first apprehended. The flag was wrested away from Jerry, and as he struggled with state troopers to keep hold of it, the flagpole was used to pummel him on the head, giving him an open bleeding wound while he was dragged to the paddy wagon.

At this point, some folks started stepping out of the line of the march onto the grass beside the curb to avoid being arrested. It was mass confusion with now-resistant marchers being hit and dragged ruthlessly down the street amid angry shouting.

In this chaos, Ned said he momentarily, without a word to anyone else, took stock within himself and decided that this was the moment of truth for him: he was going to be arrested. He had been a good way back in the line of marchers, and, standing firm in the street to show his allegiance to the cause, he was quickly grabbed by state troopers, dragged along, and shoved into a paddy wagon. As it happened, this was the same paddy wagon that already held Jerry Pogue. It was at that instant that the journalist asked Ned if he had any comment. Then my husband felt compelled to deliver his unabashed statement.

The police seemed to have earmarked this specific paddy wagon for people they deemed particularly offensive, because just before the vehicle pulled off to jail, some police officer opened the back door a crack and shot Mace into the packed space inside. The officer then quickly slammed the door shut again. The noxious, stinging teargas made the occupants nauseatingly dizzy, and their eyes felt as if on fire from the caustic chemical. And when we reconnected with Jerry Pogue forty years later, he still carried a large scar on his left cheek where the shot of Mace had seared across his skin.

When the paddy wagons reached the Prichard jail, the marchers were removed from the vehicles, shoved inside the building, searched, and then pushed into small cells. When police officers came to Ned, the only white face in the mix, they were perplexed. They talked with each other about where to put him in the racially segregated jail. Somehow they didn't see Ned as deserving to be incarcerated in the white section. And so they concluded that they would "put him in with his friends" in the segregated black section, to our good fortune.

Cells built for a maximum of two prisoners were crammed with about twenty or so people each. The Mace on people's clothing in these confined spaces quickly became unpleasantly toxic. The strong fumes from the teargas caused people to become ill and pass out.

News of what was going on traveled like wildfire through the small jail. Everyone in and around the area knew what had happened at the march, including the already incarcerated inmates. Because Ned had been the only white person arrested, his situation was prominently talked about. His actions and words had inflamed racial sentiment beyond belief in a broad swath of southern Alabama, and especially in the Prichard jail. So if my husband had been locked up in the white section of the segregated jail, it would be perfectly reasonable to think that racist inmates might well have beaten him, if not outright tried to kill him. It is the only time in my life I have ever been grateful for segregated facilities.

The retelling of the arrest story finally finished. We were all exhausted as Judy made plans for our sleeping arrangements. She and Arnie went out of their way to make us comfortable, even taking the mattress off their bed and putting it on the floor for us, as they slept on the box spring in another room. I couldn't believe their great kindness also included special attention for our wonderful yet overactive Dalmatian, Tallulah.

Sleep was difficult that night. As we lay there on the mattress, every strange noise caused my mind to picture horrible scenes like Ned being burned up before my eyes. Pushing sleep away, we talked about what might be next for us.

The church situation held huge questions. Earlier in the evening, Arnie had gotten a call from Robert Carr, the local Lutheran pastor who also served as the volunteer leader of the local clergymen in the Lutheran denomination, which both Ned and Arnie belonged to. Robert had a very specific purpose for his call. To be clear, the purpose did not include one ounce of concern over Ned's well-being. Rather, Robert asked Arnie to "suggest" that Ned mail in his resignation as pastor of Holy Cross Lutheran Church. Robert believed Ned's behavior had set off the very real possibility of vicious racial backlash that would target both the congregation and the building of Holy Cross Lutheran Church. So Robert thought the church would be much better off with Ned out of the picture completely. It was as though Robert wanted my husband to just disappear off the planet.

Robert's call proved that news of Ned's actions had traveled very fast. The man didn't even live in Mobile County, yet within a few brief hours after the arrest, Robert had felt the need to try to erase Ned's presence from the greater Lutheran community. Not surprisingly, though, Ned was not at all willing to go along with Robert's "suggestion," at least not then.

As far as what the future held for me, I knew I wanted to continue my work at the welfare department if Ned's actions had not done anything to put that part of my life in jeopardy. I also knew I was lying next to a man who had just acquired a huge target on his back. How that target would affect my life, I had no idea, but I knew the consequences would certainly touch me in some way or another.

Lying there as the early light of morning slipped into the room, I understood how foolish it would be for us go back to our house on Merritt Drive for any length of time ever again. That house was no longer our home. And as life moved on, we never did spend another night in that place I had grown to love.

CHAPTER FIFTEEN

Arrest Aftermath

Thursday morning, I returned to work. I didn't know how I was supposed to go about living my life after the events of the day before, so I just went off to my job wanting everything there to be normal, just as if nothing had happened. I was hoping the Mobile County welfare department was going to take all the stuff surrounding my husband's arrest in stride. And at least on this first day back, no one except my boss, John, even made a comment about the situation. As for his thoughts, John assured me he would be supportive of whatever I needed to do in the next few days and weeks.

I was looking to my job to provide me with an artificially safe place to be each day, while, in contrast, my husband was running around trying to connect with people who were busy distancing themselves from him.

His first priority was to try to schedule a meeting with the church's voter assembly to see if he still had a job as pastor of the church. This task proved to be extraordinarily difficult, however. He did not go into his church office, because a trashy old pickup truck was almost continually parked in the lot adjacent to the church driveway. There were two grubby-looking men in the front seat with a small arsenal of weapons hanging in the gun rack behind their heads. The parking lot was part of a doctor's office complex, and it would seem the truck just went unnoticed by the property owners. No one appeared interested in having it moved, including the police. And to be clear, the truck exuded a threatening aura parked all by itself facing the entrance to Holy Cross Lutheran Church not more than fifty feet away.

By Friday night, Ned had come up with a plan for us to leave Mobile for a few days to scout out some new job opportunities. We needed to pick up a couple of things from the parsonage for the trip, but we had to rely on trusted friends to check out the house and street first. They kept an eye out for odd vehicles or old pickup trucks with prominent gun racks parked around the neighborhood, which would have indicated possible Klan threats for us. So when all was clear, we would sneak into our house quickly and retrieve what we needed for the next few days. I was continually watching out for potential danger lurking in otherwise everyday actions, and anytime I was with my husband, my senses to possible violence became heightened.

We packed up a few things and left our sweet Tallulah with Judy and Arnie. Early the next morning, we started off for Frankfort, Kentucky. A friend had told Ned that he had heard of a job opening in the Equal Rights Division of the Kentucky State Department. After stopping in Frankfort, we planned to drive to Atlanta so Ned could meet with people from American Friends Service Committee and interview for a job with them.

I felt great relief as our car sped north away from Mobile, as though we were leaving the scene of a terrible catastrophe. I could finally breathe deeply again. In my twenty-five years, I had never known such turmoil and had certainly never expected such a scenario.

Since the arrest, I was, at times, overwhelmed with worry. When I would try to talk to Ned about it, he would change the direction of the conversation, pointing out that these kinds of difficult experiences had to happen to change the status quo surrounding racial intolerance. He would tell me again and again that, for the most part, righting injustices required sacrifice. Then he would go on about how people don't change because they wake up one morning and just decide to look at life in a more humane, loving way. They usually have to be forcibly pushed into seeing a more fair and just way of living. Finally, my husband would tell me, some people need to sacrifice to make that change happen, and it was his turn.

Well, all the rhetoric sounded very righteous in the safe confines of our car as it sped away, but back in Mobile, the same words left a lot to be desired for me. And besides, I just couldn't get past the sense of betrayal I felt. The tension continued between us as the miles flew by.

Frankfort, Kentucky, was a quiet little place, and we soon found a Holiday Inn where we could spend a few nights. Ned talked with state department officials and did the preliminary paperwork on a job application. Then we drove on to Atlanta where he met with American Friends Service Committee staff.

On the drive to Atlanta, Ned talked about another possibility. If the church wanted him to resign, he thought it would be a good idea to stay in Mobile anyway and return to school. Although he had eight years of college-level and postgrad work behind him, he had never really put the specific coursework together to acquire an official bachelor's degree. Ned knew that a degree would be essential for many future job opportunities, such as teaching. And without question, he felt that staying in Mobile would send a message to the community of his sustained commitment to civil rights issues.

The idea of staying in Mobile and demonstrating that anonymous threats would not scare us off was extremely unsettling to me, at least at first. As we drove, though, something inside me resonated with the moral value of that choice. I didn't like the idea of terrorist bullies having control of my decisions. To be honest, though, I was finding myself out of my comfort zone as the concept grew more and more acceptable to me. Maybe it wasn't the smartest decision to make, but after considerable contemplation, staying in Mobile, at least for a while, really did seem to me the right thing to do.

On the way back from Atlanta, I ultimately came to the belief that we could stay in Mobile and adjust our lives in ways that might minimize the threats. Those few days away had given me enough distance to see things a little differently. What a gift that trip was. But not to put too fine a point on it, I still possessed a great deal of anger over my feelings of betrayal.

When we returned, the Cormier family from the church offered us a safe, temporary place to stay in their home. They had more space than Judy and Arnie, and so moving into their house made sense. The Cormiers were even willing to take our confused and excitable dog—what friends.

During this period, time and again, amazing people put their lives on the line for us, and I will be eternally grateful for their courage. Amarant and Norm Cormier had three young sons living at home, so the offer to give us a place to stay was especially kind, as they were willing to put their children at risk for what they believed to be the right thing.

Both the Voigts and the Cormiers received hateful anonymous phone calls threatening their lives for their willingness to take Ned and me into their homes. They were not exempt from the widespread feelings of hatred.

Tension had heated up as news of the arrest and Ned's statement to the press had been widely reported in *JET* magazine, local and regional news outlets, and even in the *Chicago Tribune*. The backlash against Ned's arrest and his impetuous comment was strong. While people might have seen his arrest as heroic, his risky statement, "I am sick of being white," caused many moderates to join in the angry hysteria against him. Among other things, Ned was decried as "an outside agitator" and "Northern n*****-lover" on local radio and in news accounts. It mattered to only a very few that he had been a legitimate, tax-paying resident of the city for over two years and was not, therefore, an outside agitator—an agitator, maybe, but not an outsider. Further, although Ned took great exception over use of the offensive noun, "n*****," the second word in the phrase, "lover," actually precisely expressed his sentiments toward folks of other races. So the accusations against him were not entirely unfounded.

There was no master plan—no road map on how to live through a situation where you were, for the most part, considered a social pariah. I was unaware of any practical list of how-to-survive tips when dark, unknown forces seemed stacked against you. Great literary pieces and religious books have discussed in depth the human condition that results from these challenging kinds of experiences, but, as far as practical advice goes, I found very little. So I just did the best I could with what intuitive feelings I could pull up from some place inside. I met each day with an overwhelming measure of caution and just tried to get on with things. At work, I plugged along pretending like nothing had happened. It gave me a sense of peace, which was comforting since we hadn't felt safe enough to even live in our own home since the day of the arrest.

Because we were no longer living in the parsonage, and Ned was rarely at his office due to the armed pickup truck close by, my husband found it difficult to connect with people in his congregation. Pastor Robert Carr, leader of the local Lutheran clergymen in the greater Mobile area, had demanded Ned's resignation the day of the arrest. When Ned returned Robert's phone call, Robert told my husband again he wanted his letter of resignation from Holy Cross Lutheran Church. Even better, Carr said, would be a second letter of resignation from the larger church body, the Lutheran Church—Missouri Synod. Robert was especially clear he did not want the two letters personally delivered to his office or home, even though he lived only a few miles away. Instead, he insisted that Ned send the letters via US mail. It would seem that Pastor Robert Carr did not even want to be in proximity to Ned for fear he might accidentally be caught in the shadow of the target on Ned's back. He was only interested in having Ned's name and presence spectacularly disappear from anything having to do with Lutherans in the greater Mobile area.

On the other hand, Southern District offices for the Lutheran Church—Missouri Synod were located in New Orleans where the president of the district, Pastor David Hancock, had loose oversight over all the churches under his supervision, including those in Mobile. Through Arnie, Hancock contacted Ned and congregation members at Holy Cross to notify them he was calling a meeting to discuss the tense situation.

So Hancock plucked up his courage and came to Mobile to meet with voter assembly members and Ned at the church. Not very many voter assembly members showed up to the meeting, as people were understandably intimidated by the continuing aura of threats surrounding Ned. At the meeting, Ned was given the opportunity under the surprisingly supportive leadership of Southern District officials to present his rationale for why he had done what he had done. His reason was uncomplicated: it was the right thing to do following Christian precepts of justice. The meeting took an unlikely turn when Hancock stated that if he had the power to keep Ned in his current position at Holy Cross, he would do so, validating Ned's actions. But the Lutheran church governance system gave all power for these decisions directly to local congregations. So the Southern District president had no final say on the issue whatsoever.

When a church vote was taken on whether to accept Ned's resignation, the result was remarkably close: the all-male voter assembly members voted six to five to accept Ned's resignation. So just six days after his arrest for parading without a permit, Ned was officially out of a job as pastor of Holy Cross Lutheran Church. My husband was now without an income, and we were without a home.

What happened next in our lives was the arrival of unexpected gifts of loving kindness and generosity without measure. The black community's commitment to creating a safe and welcoming place for Ned and me became amazingly apparent. My husband had become a larger-than-life folk hero to most black citizens around Mobile County who reveled in what was considered his astoundingly brave behavior on the day of the march. So after signing for his bail, the supportive community planned to help us find a more secure home and then orchestrate our move.

Friends had information for us on some inexpensive houses that were available through the University of South Alabama. We went to look at one with three small bedrooms and one bath; it was not quite a thousand square feet, and it was close to the university campus. Best of all, it was located in a community made up entirely of black families.

The developer had overbuilt, so about one-fourth of the homes in the tract remained empty. The university had bought up these empty homes with long-term plans to eventually expand the campus's perimeter to include the acreage. But the homes were available as rentals for the foreseeable future, costing a reasonable sixty-five dollars a month. The place was sunny, clean, and well maintained, and most importantly it met the safe location test. Tallulah even had a wonderful yard. It was so much better than I had even hoped for.

After we signed rental papers for the house, two friends who lived in the new community quickly stepped up to help us move. The parsonage was frequently being watched by malevolent forces, so the moving plan had to be carefully thought out. Around dusk a day or two later, two future neighbors who happened to own trucks, James and Amos, arrived at our old house on Merritt Drive. Ned and these two men, along with Arnie, Judy, and I, slipped into the house and started to organize our belongings, hastily throwing things into boxes and bags. We worked quickly, always watching for unannounced threatening people to show up. But thankfully, nothing like that happened.

Amos had left the truck down the street a bit, but at nightfall he backed it up the driveway to the carport. It didn't take us long to load our furniture and personal belongings onto the truck. We used only flashlights, as turning lights on in the home would have given those who wished us harm a better view.

As a final farewell to the church-owned home, Judy and I wrapped a strip of clean tissue paper around the toilet seat to show it had been "sanitized" for the next occupants. We liked to think that, even in the tense moments of the situation, fear had not taken our sense of humor. In reality, though, that thought was unsustainable.

Our last few hours in the parsonage were a sharp contrast to the celebratory welcome that had occurred less than two years before when Ned and I had first arrived. Driving away for the last time, I struggled with mixed feelings: sadness over the loss of a dream, and excitement for a new, safer place to live. Two years before, we had found a sweet, inviting home and a successful life as pastor and wife. That life had now been exchanged for an existence where our energies were challenged because we were living outside the mainstream. I didn't realize at the time, though, that it was not going to be such a bad trade-off, after all.

Driving the fifteen minutes in the dark to the new house, we were careful to check to see if anyone was following our little caravan. We breathed a big collective sigh of relief when we were pretty sure no one was. The same group of friends helped us unload our belongings, this time with a little more care. The black community provided us with a far safer backdrop than the white community we had just left ever would have.

When we were about finished, a neighbor from down the street showed up to welcome us. A fit-looking man of about forty, wearing a T-shirt and jeans, Titus Jasper had a small piece of paper tightly gripped in his hand. Pulling Ned aside, Titus spoke in a soft, muffled voice. At the end of the short conversation, he handed the paper to Ned. I thought Titus must be a night owl, as he was still up and aware of what was happening in his neighborhood around midnight, the time of our move-in. Little did I know that he was part of the unofficial neighborhood watch group that was always alert, and which now felt responsible for our safety, too.

I had been thinking about how I wanted to arrange our furniture in the new place, so the plan I had in my head took shape quickly as the pieces came through the door. A little after midnight, we finally finished moving everything in, including Tallulah. And once again we were indebted to courageous friends for their generous help.

After everyone left, Ned and I stood in the kitchen savoring our new home with a sense of peace I hadn't felt for several days. I indulged myself with the happy thought that maybe our hopes were going to come true. Maybe Ned and I could create a life here in Mobile that would provide satisfaction and even joy to us both again.

Then Ned pulled out the piece of paper Titus Jasper had given him earlier. He was very pleased to show me the names of community volunteers on the list, all of whom lived close by. Next to each name was a telephone number. Titus had instructed Ned to keep the list in a safe place, because each person on the list owned guns, and "in case of trouble of any kind, like a cross burning on your front lawn or anything else like that," they would come immediately when called to help.

Ned slid the paper into the tiny space between the wall and the phone. The paper remained in that spot next to the phone for the next twelve months—as long as we lived in the house. Looking at that piece of paper, I understood what a critical element it was in our whole surreal experience. I again had a sense of safety, even though this time it was to be provided by a vigilante group.

I stared at Ned. Amazingly, he seemed nonchalant, filled with eagerness and confidence. But it came to me again that our decision to stay in Mobile for the foreseeable future would continue to be full of uncertainty. What I didn't count on was the immense preponderance of grace I was to find in this future. Standing there in our new kitchen, a feeling of peace came over me. We were no longer alone in this strange, unforgiving place. People who cared were looking out for us, and we were going to be all right.

CHAPTER SIXTEEN

Sunday-Morning Church

Ned soon found a part-time job with an anti-poverty organization funded by the Catholic Church, where he worked to improve the lives of poor people living on the city dump. The effort brought him a great sense of satisfaction. He also registered for classes for the fall semester at the University of South Alabama to finish course work on a teaching credential in math and science.

To our surprise, Ned and I discovered that when we left the new house, our neighbors were frequently kind of just hanging around. Folks seemed excited to meet Ned and talk to him face-to-face. It would appear his folk-hero reputation had preceded him. And the daily conversations with people in the community soon led to invitations for Ned to preach at gospel churches on Sunday mornings. The idea of spending Sunday morning in church with new friends and neighbors was exciting for me because I missed the feeling of community that had been part of my usual Sunday-morning church life before Ned's arrest.

The first invitation was for a Sunday morning in July at a Baptist church located in a black community near Prichard. Ned and I woke up early and dressed quickly. I wore my favorite sleeveless A-line gray-and-cream paisley dress. And I would never have thought of going to church without gloves and a hat at that time. Ned knew the clerical collar could sometimes be perceived as stuffy, so instead he wore his dark suit, a white shirt, and a tie. He wanted to be sure that people wouldn't be put off by his appearance. He looked quite handsome and self-confidant as I caught a long glimpse of him getting into the car.

We arrived early at the small square building with a church steeple perched precariously on the roof. A proud sign in front announced the church name, and the name of the pastor, Henry Williams. Sitting on a tiny piece of land amid small houses and storefronts, time had taken its toll on the building, which had been constructed with minimal financial resources. But devoted parishioners had planted bright-red zinnias and sunny marigolds around the front entrance for a warm, inviting feeling. The weathered white clapboard exterior was in need of paint and basic maintenance, but the structure itself gave off a surprising vitality that seemed tied directly to the solid red Alabama dirt upon which it stood.

I had always loved gospel music, and so the morning had promise to be a really neat experience, even though the oppressive heat began to dampen my excitement a little. As was usual in most public spaces, the church had no air conditioning, but large old windows had been thrown open to entice in any wandering coastal breezes.

Front doors had been propped open wide, and inside were women and men of all shapes and sizes dressed in immaculately clean, well-pressed, mostly homespun attire, quite surely the very best clothes they owned. Women had taken great care choosing lovely and interesting hats—a staple then for good church ladies all over the area. Most of the colorful hats were adorned with floppy silk flowers and tasteful netting surrounding huge brims.

Color-coordinated gloves and shoes added a real downtown feeling to the outfits.

Laughing children hopped around tugging on adults' hands, while smiling faces gave off an engaging sense of welcome, and soft chuckles bubbled happily below the greetings. The churchgoers' delight of having Ned, the area's new folk hero, right there among them was palpable. It had not stopped surprising me that my courageous and outspoken husband had become a rather first-class celebrity in certain places. Although the excitement over my husband was fun to watch, I didn't have to dig too deep inside myself to unearth layers of anger toward him over the fact that his brash behavior had turned my life into rather a fear-infested mess. But my problems were not on anyone's mind that morning.

Woven loosely through the hot humid air were fragrances like lily of the valley perfume and Yardley English lavender soap. The sweet scents hung lovingly on my clothes as I was hugged close by one woman after another. Somehow, I felt as though I had mysteriously been transported to an endearing place in my grandparents' living room in Wooster, Ohio. My rather common companion—anxiety—seemed to disappear as I experienced openhearted joy washing over me from those warm hugs.

Inside the church sanctuary, paint was peeling and hanging off in some places in small, uneven strips. Church pews were set in a semicircle around the front platform. Open areas around the outside perimeter held spotty collections of old wooden folding chairs.

A tall, genteel-looking older man in a well-worn suit, a white shirt, and a tie introduced himself to me as Pastor Henry Williams. He seemed openly pleased that Ned was actually at his church, and he was kind about me being there with my husband.

In the front of the sanctuary, on either side, were two flags—a US flag and a Christian flag. Behind the pulpit and between the flags were two almost throne-like chairs. Pastor Williams guided Ned up to one of the chairs, and then he sat down in the other.

Two of the ladies I had been talking with took my arm and gently nudged me into one of the front-row pews next to them.

Sitting quietly for a few moments before church started, my mind leaped to a narrative I had recently heard about. The story described a group of African tribespeople who had been kidnapped and forced aboard the *Clotilde*, the last known slave ship from Africa. It was a horrifying account of over one hundred victimized people aboard that infamous ship that landed in Mobile Bay in 1859.

The ship owner knew the souls on his ship could not be legally enslaved because of the 1807 law that prohibited importing slaves, but he had believed—on a bet—that he could sneak in under the eye of the federal government and illegally dispose of his cargo in the underground slave market anyway. This act proved to be more difficult than he had planned. The human cargo from the ship was then secretly distributed in the dark of night to opportunists who treated these kidnapped souls as chattel rather than human beings.

The remarkable part of this tale was that about thirty members of this woeful group who had not been literally given away were ultimately turned out on a remote section of land along Mobile Bay at Magazine Point. Here on this forlorn corner of the earth, thousands of miles from their homeland in a place where no one spoke their language, and governed by people who despised them, they were left to fend for themselves with no food, potable water, clothing, shelter, or protection. Descendants of the amazing survivors of this horrific event still reside on this incredible piece of land now known as Africatown, a nearby neighborhood of Mobile. And as I sat there on that Sunday morning, I wondered if some of the descendants of this miraculous group of people might possibly be right there in the sanctuary with me. What an overwhelmingly humbling thought it was.

As people began to take their places in the sanctuary, it occurred to me I was watching an extraordinary ballet. In the opening scene, Pastor Williams began to arrange papers on the pulpit. At the venerable baby grand piano, a middle-aged woman with wispy gray hair started to play gospel hymns with incredible ease. Her simple, demure white dress puddled loosely around her on the piano bench. Playing without music, her whole body swayed with the luxurious sounds that rose from the old, quite stately instrument.

Next, I watched as groups of people gathered in areas where there were wooden folding chairs; one seemed to be a children's section, another a section for teens, and two others for adult members. It quickly became apparent that each group was a separate choir. With so many folks gathering in these choir groups, it left only a few of us sitting in the main sanctuary. But the resulting music was fabulous: "This Little Light of Mine" sung by the children's choir, then "Swing Low Sweet Chariot," followed by the haunting favorite, "We'll Understand It By and By" sung by the adult choirs.

The lyrics of "We'll Understand It By and By" struck me with its prayerfully haunting words:

> We are tossed and driven on the restless sea
> of time
> Somber skies and howling tempests oft succeed
> a bright sunshine
> In that land of perfect day, when the mists
> have rolled away
> We'll understand it by and by
>
> By and by when the morning comes
> When the saints of God are gathered home
> We'll tell the story how we've overcome
> For we'll understand it by and by

Bible readings, prayers, and announcements were spaced out between the various choir selections. Everyone seemed to want to be a part of the awesome music with hand clapping and foot stomping. One after another would step forward and sing an incredible solo. Each choir amped up the energy level until the room felt alive with the fervor of an old-fashioned revival meeting. I forgot about the heat and just luxuriated in the music. I recalled so many happy memories of my own religious musical history in the Baptist church, a drab distant cousin to the current experience but a cousin nonetheless.

When it came time for Ned to speak, the sanctuary became very quiet. In introducing Ned, Pastor Williams talked about his recent arrest and his controversial comment to the press. He said Ned was a trusted, dear friend who showed courage "when the chips were down." Williams told the congregation how proud he was to have "this amazing Christian minister" in his church.

Ned spoke to the congregation about the infinite value of each human being. He was good at helping people feel God's love at work within each person. During the sermon, the sanctuary was peppered with "amen," "thank you, Jesus," and "hallelujah," along with other emotional comments from worshipers. I loved every moment of it.

After Ned's talk, Pastor Williams thanked him warmly and then asked the congregation to dig deeply into their pockets because he wanted to present a monetary gift of love to Ned from the church. As the offering plates were passed, the pastor encouraged participants to give with a generous heart. This offering was in addition to the regular offering for the church, so it was in essence a second offering during the same church service. People seemed eager to contribute their "love gifts" to honor this man that they felt had acted so bravely on their behalf. They knew Ned had lost his job because of the arrest, and they wanted to contribute economically. I was taken aback by this act of generosity. It was totally unexpected. It was difficult for me to consider accepting monetary gifts from folks who had so very little themselves. But not accepting it might seem to be an insult to their generosity.

After church, members were eager for us to stay for a planned meal. In a small room off the back of the sanctuary, tables had been set up and were topped with platters and dishes full of fried chicken, fish, potato salad, collard greens, peach cobbler, and wonderful sweet potato pie. Sitting down to the meal, I felt as though I was in the home of good friends whom I had known all my life. The whole experience radiated generosity, and gratitude. But without question, the feelings flowed both ways. I was very beholden for the extraordinary love that had been shown to me that day.

Other invitations to preach at gospel congregations followed, and we spent most every Sunday morning for several weeks in similar churches across the city. But only the marginalized black church groups who had the combination of financial independence and courage invited Ned to their places of worship. Black churches with a major connection to a mainstream religious denomination did not seem to want to risk offending the white power structure that often supported them economically by inviting my controversial husband to speak. Or maybe those congregations just didn't want to sit through a sermon by Ned Milner. Either way, the invitations didn't come from that direction.

After our first experience with the monetary love offering, Ned and I talked about how uncomfortable we were accepting that kind of gift. Even though our income was tight, we agreed we would return each offering, anonymously, however we could, so as not to seem unappreciative. It really was unthinkable that we do anything else.

But the church experiences within the black community that summer and fall of 1968 remain imprinted on my memory as beacon-like images of the new social order we had become a part of—a world of extraordinary kindness, generosity, and love that enfolded our lives in continually surprising ways.

CHAPTER SEVENTEEN

Prichard Court Hearing

Ned's audacious, in-your-face attitude never showed cracks. There was nothing in him that questioned what he had said and done the day of the Prichard job march. He avoided talking with me about the arrest, telling me it was his business, not mine. In his playbook, it came down to the fact that if I couldn't be a mindless cheerleader, I was supposed to keep quiet and stay out of his way. Although I was furious over the threatened danger we lived in, for the most part I kept my mouth shut. So taking time off work to go to Ned's court hearing didn't occur to me. I was now the major breadwinner of the family, after all, and had already missed a good deal of work related to Ned's arrest drama anyway.

A few weeks after the Prichard march, the day for Ned's preliminary hearing dawned bright. The one-hundred-plus people who had been arrested together in Prichard on June 12 were scheduled to appear in Prichard's recorder's court before Judge Robert Vickers. This large group had been split into four smaller groups, with each smaller group summoned to court on a different day. City officials saw it as an effort to try to prevent the possibility of more civil unrest if the whole group of about one hundred showed up all at one time. No one knew what to expect from Judge Vickers, but tensions were high. Ned's name was on the list of the first group scheduled to appear.

To be clear, Ned was never the official or unofficial leader of this group, nor had he ever been seen as any kind of leader of the Prichard march. But because he was the only white person arrested on that day, the white power structure of the city of Prichard saw things differently. Apparently, to them a white man automatically—without question—meant organizer/leader.

The recorder's court was the only courtroom in the Prichard city hall building. Large enough to accommodate the arrestees, lawyers, and other assorted folks, the utilitarian space was full of a collection of cast-off tables and chairs. In the front was a sturdy desk-type bench flanked on each side by state of Alabama and US flags.

Court was called to order by the bailiff. Judge Vickers, an older man dressed in less-than-impressive-looking judicial robes, had a short fringe of gray hair from ear to ear around the back of his skull, leaving an otherwise shiny head. And when he spoke, his voice came out of his small frame with a scratchy Southern drawl.

After the judge took his seat, the bailiff arranged the group of arrestees in one long single line stretched out in front of the bench. One by one, the bailiff called each name, and that person would step forward. Then the judge would raise his head, squint his eyes from behind his wire-frame glasses, and in his raspy voice, sternly say, "You are fined fifty dollars for parading without a permit." Then the arrestee would be motioned back into the line again.

The fifty-dollar fines shocked people. Fifty dollars was a great deal of money, especially for poor people who, if they had a job at all, were certainly in very low income brackets. These folks had simply nonviolently continued a march that had originally been permitted by the city. The only violence that was perpetrated had been by the police against the marchers. There was no discussion regarding innocence or guilt, no talk of a jury trial, just the outrageous fifty-dollar fine meted out to each marcher.

The clock ticked along with each person rhythmically stepping forward until Ned's name came up. When Ned's given name, George E. Milner Jr., was read, Judge Vickers paused. His face pulled into a hot red mass of taut muscles as he lowered his head to look over the top of his glasses. When Ned stepped forward, Judge Vickers began an angry tirade that unnerved most everyone in the room.

The judge wanted everyone to know that he considered Ned to be one of the leaders in the Prichard march. The judge was unambiguous that he had made this assumption, not based on any evidence, but rather on the fact that Ned had white skin. And because Ned was, therefore, seen as a leader, he should bear a heavier responsibility for what the judge believed to be the "outrageous behavior" of so many citizens on that day. Ned was then given a one-hundred-dollar fine and fifteen days in jail for parading without a permit, behavior the judge believed had incited "great civil unrest" in the city of Prichard.

The judge went on to say, "Outsiders like George Milner are not welcome in Prichard." Then the judge elaborated on the theory that he believed Ned should know, as everyone did, that "Negroes have a lower mental capacity, and are capable of easily being led." Therefore, in Judge Vickers's estimation, Ned was one of the core leaders essentially responsible for the entire ill-fated Prichard march.

As the judge paused for a moment, Ned spoke up with the question, "What makes you think I was a leader?" Judge Vickers did not respond.

Right after the hearing, all the arrestees were quickly taken into custody again and were ushered out of city hall to be once more incarcerated in the Prichard jail. They were informed that they were being locked up a second time until bail could be posted, again. Outside, friends and family gathered. Everyone was uneasy and upset over how things had gone with the ridiculously high fines and reincarceration. The NAACP lawyer tried to reassure people by telling them the case would be appealed. But the current state of affairs, with twenty-three people behind bars again, was extraordinarily tense.

Without question, the white power structure of Prichard had done some behind-the-scenes strategizing before the preliminary hearing. As family and friends tried to work within the system to obtain bail, they soon found out the only bail bonds company licensed in Prichard outright refused to work with anyone to post bail for any of the Prichard march arrestees now in jail. The company would give no reason for the denial. And to show how particularly mean-spirited Prichard city officials were, Judge Vickers would not allow any other bail bond company from the nearby city of Mobile to work with people to post bail, either. So city manipulation of the bail bond process prevented citizens from obtaining bail in community-accepted ways.

There was, then, no clear path to get these people released on that hot afternoon in July. Fortunately, Ned once again found himself rather safely incarcerated on the black side of the segregated jail, but, nonetheless, he and his fellow marchers were still behind bars.

After a good deal of time and effort, Arnie and other civil rights activists finally rounded up three black property owners who promised to sign an appeal oath to fund the bail for all the incarcerated folks. But the whole process was shaky, as people were extremely fearful of the heavy-handed demonstrations of "justice" Prichard city officials had just dished out to the marchers.

I had been at work all day and was unaware of what was going on. After work, I thought I should stop by Prichard city hall to catch up on what had happened at the hearing. Arnie saw me and filled me in. He told me he didn't know how long it would take to come to some kind of resolution on the bail issue. Sitting there in my car, in the same place I had been just a few weeks before, brought back vividly scary memories of the day of the arrest for me. But this time, I didn't feel the need to try to have some eye contact with Ned through the bars as I had the last time. I simply sat there feeling as though I had fallen into the middle of another bad dream.

Arnie said I should go home and wait for the bail process to unfold. It was a welcome decision for me at that moment. At least I would be going home to a community of neighbors who would be there for me, unlike the last time. So I drove off to wait for Ned's release with my trusty companion, Tallulah.

As the process to establish a bail bond fund continued, one of the three property owners who had originally agreed decided to back out. It took until about ten o'clock in the evening for Arnie and the other activists to finally persuade this last homeowner to sign on the appeal bond so the rearrested marchers could be bailed out.

In the meantime, the later it got, more tempers were fraying in the neighborhoods of Prichard. Friends and families were finding out about what had happened at the preliminary hearing, including the incredible refusal of the local bail bond company to post bail. The community was incensed. A group of infuriated people met at Reverend Ray's church, the original starting point of the Prichard march. Hostility over the high-handed notion of justice displayed by the city of Prichard pushed folks at this meeting to angrily head over to the jail as a group to demonstrate their frustration.

At the jail, the group of folks who had been quietly waiting there for hours had just become aware of the final sign-off for the bail deal. This group had to then become a buffer between the newly arrived antagonistic protestors from the church meeting and the police department by forcibly sidetracking the protestors, persuading them to turn around and calm down. A potential bloody situation between irate citizens and police was narrowly averted. It was one a.m. before everyone was finally released and allowed to go home.

I was awake anxiously sitting on the couch with Tallulah when Ned finally came in. He wasn't in a mood to talk much about all that had happened, except to tell me quite offhandedly about his fine and jail sentence. But he was eager to have a cheese sandwich and a cup of coffee, since food had not been provided behind bars. Then he went off to bed, exhausted. I remained sitting on the couch thinking how grateful I was that I had just safely lived through another twenty-four hours in this surreal existence that had become my life.

As the NAACP attorney had promised, the case was eventually appealed to the Mobile circuit court. Ned and the *for-real* leaders of the Prichard march, Reverend Ray, Jerry Pogue, Bip Beasley, and James Dixon, all of whom had received the same one-hundred-dollar fine and fifteen days in jail, had their fines lowered to fifty dollars each to be commensurate with the others who had been arrested. And Ned's jail sentence was dropped, since it was determined he really wasn't a Prichard march organizer after all. Jail time for the actual leaders, however, was upheld.

The case eventually ended up in the US district court of Alabama with the legendary Judge Frank M. Johnson presiding. To this day, Ned and I consider it a great honor to have had this civil rights bastion of courage, Judge Johnson, rule on a case in which Ned was involved, even though the outcome did not change.

CHAPTER EIGHTEEN

Daleen Foster

We had made a conscious choice not to talk about Ned's tenuous life as a moving target for the Klan. He just never wanted to waste his time on that matter. Additionally, my husband really didn't allow fear to live in his psyche and, as usual, had little interest in my daily struggles with it. I lived in almost constant dread of an attack of some kind or another, but I did my best to stuff these kinds of thoughts. After all, I had been half the team that had made a very clear decision to stay on in Mobile after Ned's arrest. So my internal message to myself was: get over it.

Every day at work, I knew there were a good many people who continued to have thoughts of violence toward Ned, but rather naively, I felt safe. It was Ned who had been arrested, not me. That was until I got a call from the secretary of the Mobile County welfare department's director, Daleen Foster. The call from her secretary told me to come to Foster's office the next day for a meeting.

Ms. Foster, a highly respected member of the community, came from a well-to-do, old guard Mobile family. She had served as director of the Mobile County welfare department for many years and was considered a powerful inside member of the elite group of community leaders in the Mobile County political scene.

Although I had worked for the department for about a year, I'd never met Ms. Foster. Her office was in downtown Mobile, and the office where I worked, Zelda's Place, was farther out from the center of the city. I was struck with a bit of apprehension regarding the call because the secretary had just said, "Ms. Foster wants you to come in and see her"—end of conversation. I could think of nothing that I'd done that would be considered inappropriate or unprofessional. In fact, I'd recently been assigned to special intensive-care cases that were given to just a few of the more trusted caseworkers.

The next day, I drove downtown to the meeting wondering what was going on. Ms. Foster's secretary opened the door to her spacious, well-appointed office and stepped back, waving her hand toward the opening. I was drawn in by the sound of Foster's voice, heavily flavored with a rich Southern inflection. But her words jolted me. With great authority, she said to me, "Mrs. Milner, come in and close the door behind you, because if you repeat any of this conversation outside this room, *I will deny every word of it.*" At that moment, I knew I was in for a bumpy ride.

I closed the door, anxiously looking in her direction. I didn't have a clue what this was all about, but I certainly knew enough already to predict it wasn't going to be a feel-good meeting. Daleen Foster, sitting serenely behind her picture-perfect desk, was a large woman in her late forties, beautifully dressed in a pastel plaid linen suit with coordinated pink silk blouse. Lifting her well-manicured hand, she pointed a finger to a cushy-looking chair across from her desk. I walked over and sat down feeling like I had just fallen into Alice's rabbit hole in Wonderland. With a cold and particularly unnerving smile, she looked across the desk at me. A long silence followed, as if she wanted to assure herself no other ears were going to be hearing her. The whole room was saturated with imperiousness, and I became more uncomfortable as time ticked away.

Her next words to me were stunning. "Mrs. Milner, I called you in today because I happen to know that the Ku Klux Klan is well aware of the territory you are now assigned to in the northern end of the county as a caseworker. They are also aware you drive on unpopulated back roads alone every week performing your assigned job duties. You are, therefore, an easy target for them."

Well, she certainly wasted no time with small talk or pleasantries; instead, she'd just leaped right into the heart of the matter. Continuing even more slowly and with greater emphasis, she then said, "Because I don't happen to want your blood on my hands, I am reassigning you to another territory in the department—one more centrally located."

It was as if I had been swallowed up by some huge monster and was flailing as I slid down the monster's throat. I couldn't seem to get my bearings. Unconsciously, I held my breath while she continued. "Additionally, in this new territory, your caseload will be made up mostly of white clients, unlike your current caseload. And this new caseload should give you far less opportunity to stir up problems with poor Negro folks."

My brain had fallen into a murky haze. What was I hearing? I tried to process her words, but the haze just continued to cloud my thinking, making me unable to speak.

Then she paused again, this time for several moments. It was at this point that a question popped into my head: Was I supposed to thank her for something? What I had just heard was her attempt to lessen any guilt she might feel should something happen to me at the hands of the Klan. Really, was I to thank her for that? Or should I have self-righteously marched out of her office protesting her false accusations of my presumed subversive behavior organizing poor black welfare clients? Maybe someone had reported the incident with Addie Mae at the infirmary in Saraland to her; I don't know. But clearly Daleen Foster perceived me as a troublemaker, in addition to being married to a first-rate rabble-rouser.

Thinking about my response to the pause didn't take very long, though, since fear pretty much dictated that I choose the first option, that of expressing appreciation for her thoughtfulness in reassigning me. Somehow my mouth stammered out a weak, "Thank you."

Ms. Foster offered no connecting of the dots as to how she knew what she did about the Klan. And I never pushed aside my brain haze enough to ask her about this important issue.

Foster then prattled on, telling me she had already taken care of the reassignment detail—ya-de-ya-de-ya. Sitting there with a rather smug look on her face, she contentedly believed she had washed her hands of any responsibility she might have had for my safety. Job done, reassignment complete, dismissed. *Oh, and don't let the door hit you on the way out.*

Driving back to work after the meeting, I thought what incredible insight I'd just had into the interior thinking of a major city figure. She had admitted to me firsthand knowledge of the Klan's retaliation plans. She clearly had some contact with those notorious terrorists. I was appalled over how deeply woven into the mainstream fabric of the community the Klan really was.

Another disturbing thought now took control of my brain. After this meeting with Foster, I knew my life was very likely as much at risk as Ned's. This turned my notion of being safe right on its head. I would never sit alone in my car again in Mobile without feeling very uneasy.

As a child, I remember my mother telling me of a vivid memory of the Klan from her own childhood when her family lived in central Florida in the 1920s. She remembered being held in her father's arms while he was standing in front of their little bungalow in Bradenton. They were witnessing a Ku Klux Klan rally in the street. It was nighttime, and Klan participants were dressed in white robe-like costumes with strange-looking pointy hoods extending down and completely covering their faces. They carried long flaming torches, and the toxic energy of the scene gave the night sky an eerie feeling. Her father told her what she was witnessing was bad and that she should never forget seeing these evil people. The episode left an indelible mark on my mother, remaining strong in her memory bank until her very last years.

I always felt a frightening chill when she would relate the Klan scene to me. My mother's tale continued to inhabit an unpleasant place in my mind, even into adulthood. And now, years after that memory she could not forget, there I was in Mobile, Alabama, experiencing my own Klan-related stories.

CHAPTER NINETEEN

Overcoming

After our move to the new community, I felt a tad more secure surrounded by kind and loyal neighbors who assured us they were willing to be there whenever we needed them. But I had, nonetheless, become accustomed to frequent thoughts of violence against both Ned and me, especially after my meeting with Daleen Foster. I found if I spent too much time on these thoughts, though, I had little energy left to do even simple things. I worried over who might be coming to attack us, or if, on some especially dark night, someone would construct a burning cross in our front yard. Some days I was a whole lot better at redirecting my anxiety than others, but for the most part, quite unconsciously, I allowed this negativity to take a central place in my psyche.

The one thing I was sure of, though, was that I wanted to teach again in the public schools. Besides the joy I had already found in teaching, I believed as a teacher I would be able to escape my current caseworker job, which was now pretty much scaring the life out of me when I was alone "in the field" doing my work. I couldn't get the idea out of my head that, according to the director of the welfare department herself, Daleen Foster, the Klan was trying to track me when I was on welfare client visits. Even though my casework area had been changed because of Foster's desire to try to keep my blood off her hands—as she so graphically put it—I still didn't feel any safer. In fact, now that I had concrete information on how vulnerable I really was, I didn't feel safe doing my job as a caseworker much at all.

Early one hot August evening, I was standing on my front lawn talking to a few neighbors who had come out, like I had, to catch some evening breezes and cool off a bit. Charlie Drum, a gregarious guy who lived a few doors down, was in the group. As it happened, he told me he was a school principal. It seemed a coincidence that he was standing there as I was telling neighbors how much I wanted to leave the welfare department and find a job teaching. I said I believed the school district had refused to hire me, maybe because of Ned's involvement in civil rights, but I didn't have any proof. I told my neighbors I believed I had the necessary experience and documentation for a teaching job, but no offer had come since I'd applied several months earlier.

Then, out of nowhere, Charlie gave me new hope, saying, "Molly, I think you should try again with another application. You need to insist on an interview, and then during the interview you should just happen to mention you're considering a civil rights law-suit against the district." Charlie continued, "You might tell them the basis of this suit would be that you're alleging discrimination because you believe many, if not all, recent hires of the district have less education, and less actual classroom experience, than you do." Charlie confidently crossed his arms over his solid chest and gently rocked back and forth as if to make his point more credible.

Although the idea of a legal challenge against the district had crossed my mind now and again, the premise seemed weak because I had no validation of my suspicions. Now Charlie Drum, an actual school district administrator, had implied there might be credible documenting information. It seemed that if I could find the back-bone to carry out Charlie's suggestion, I might possibly stand a chance of being hired after all.

Charlie's plan was first to confront the school district in an interview and then, if the district still refused to hire me, take the next step and file a formal civil rights lawsuit. While all this was settling in my brain, Charlie leaned over and said to me in a knowing voice, "Harold Moore is the man to talk to at the district office."

During a coffee break at work the next day, I looked up the school district number. I asked the operator for Harold Moore's office and was soon on the line with Miss Brogan, Moore's secretary. I told her I wanted an appointment with Mr. Moore to talk about the status of the application I had filed with the district some time back. She seemed less than happy about making the appointment, but after some pushing on my part, she gave in, and before I knew it, I had an interview for the following week.

A few days later, I took three hours of personal-leave time from my caseworker job and drove to the main office of the school district, a nondescript two-story administrative building in downtown Mobile. I pulled my little blue Opel into an empty space in the parking lot marked for visitors, then turned off the car engine. I sat there for a few minutes—windows down, soaking in the deliciously sweet aroma of nearby gardenias.

Sitting among the bushes resplendent with fragile, waxy white flowers, I reviewed again exactly what I was going to say. This was my second chance at achieving what I really wanted to do, and I didn't want to blow it. Charlie had helped me focus on the essential premise of my argument, but I had to construct my own wording. And just as important, I had to pull some courage together from who knew where to make my case sound viable.

In the midst of these mesmerizing flowers, extravagant luxuries to my Northern senses, I did some soul-searching. Could I really summon up enough bravery to confront the district with what I believed to be true? Could I really challenge an entrenched public system that had incredible power behind it, all by my silly little self? There I was, a twenty-five-year-old, naïve, pushy, Northern interloper, thinking I could take on such a ridiculously tough fight and win. How absurd. To top everything off, I seemed in denial of the basic fact that I was married to the wild-eyed social activist whose outrageous behavior had turned us both into pariahs in mainstream white Mobile circles. What the devil did I think I was going to accomplish, after all?

While I sat there stewing, the wonderful fragrance of the gardenias seemed to work a little bit of magic on me, and to my surprise, I began to feel my apprehension diminish a bit.

Allowing myself to wallow in a bit of self-doubt, I came back to the key question: *What have you got to lose anyway?* Considering the possibilities, it seemed the worst the school district could do was to throw me out of the building. And to be honest, that scenario didn't hold much dread for me after the violent threats the Klan had already made. The school district would have to come up with a more creatively nasty threat to equal anything I had already heard from white supremacists—like the idea of watching some cowardly hooded terrorist pour gasoline on my husband and set him on fire. And to my surprise, my deep-seated yearning to teach once again overcame everything else as I opened the car door, got out, and began walking toward the building.

I had chosen to wear a conservative blue linen dress. With short sleeves and a fitted waist, it buttoned up the front to a high neckline, and the A-line skirt stopped right above my knees. If looks could win the day, I thought I stood a decent chance.

Carefully tucked inside a large folder, I carried copies of my bachelor's degree from an accredited college, teaching evaluations from two Northern school districts, and teaching credentials from three states. It seemed to me that those documents should validate my credibility as an authentically trained and experienced teacher. So finally finding the optimism my grandfather had tried to instill in me, I grabbed hold of the absurd belief that I had a pretty good chance for success on this mission. This thought bolstered my fledgling rise of courage.

Armed with my official paperwork, I marched myself into the building. Searching the halls for Harold Moore's office, I found white faces everywhere I looked. There seemed to be no black employees in the main administrative offices—none. Then I saw a tall, lanky black man dressed in threadbare denim overalls and worn-out work shoes walking slowly along the hall ahead of me, a mop and bucket in hand. I felt as though I had no supporters anywhere in the building except for perhaps this custodian. But I surely didn't want to put his job at risk by making any public connection with him, so I continued quietly on my search.

Finally, I found Harold Moore's name on a door. Venturing into the outer office, the air was saturated with the essence of Southern white privilege, marked decidedly with a prominent Confederate flag showcased proudly on a filing cabinet. Sally Brogan, Moore's secretary, flitted about the room like a caged canary. Her voice flowed sugary sweet into my ears, the stickiness slowing down my synapses. I struggled to process her words. She nervously pointed at a chair, and after struggling to decipher her directive to "sit down" through the sugary morass, I sat down.

Tension from Sally's nervous behavior was extraordinary. A rather colorless, middle-aged woman with gray hair sneaking out here and there at her temples, Sally was dressed in a beige polyester suit, a stiff white blouse, and solid low-heeled shoes—very office-secretary looking. Her syrupy voice contained a distinct coldness—but my resolve remained firm. I had come this far, and a little bit of coldness wasn't going to put me off.

At last, Sally, the canary lady, escorted me into Mr. Moore's office. Entering the room, I was struck with an outsize vision of professional chaos. Mr. Moore, himself disheveled, was mild-mannered, middle-aged, and balding, with soft baby-pink cheeks. He had perhaps consumed more than his fair share of Southern cornbread, by the look of his waistline. His glasses sat low on his pudgy nose, and his white shirt under his light-gray polyester suit was badly rumpled. Mr. Moore motioned for me to sit down across the desk from him as he slowly lowered himself into his chair.

With a big smile pasted across his face and a surprisingly cheerful Southern drawl, he asked, "And now what can I do for you, little lady?" I answered as sweetly as I could, "You can offer me a teaching position with the district." Now a true Southern "little lady" would probably have slathered out a polite "sir" at the end of that statement, but both of us knew I didn't hold much credibility in that department. I knew deep down that I stood a better chance at achieving my goal if I could be perceived as much as possible as demure, gentile, and subservient, but that was a tall order for me. Mostly I saw that role as just plain demeaning. But now and again during the interview, I gave it my best effort anyway, being the desperate woman that I was.

Nervousness caused me to just leap right in, but my directness seemed to make Moore fall into a prolonged silence. This rattled my fragile self-confidence. It still didn't register in my brain how assertive my Northern voice often sounded to most homegrown people in the Deep South, even though I had been a dues-paying Southerner now for two years. Well, maybe my Northern accent was what caused Moore to clam up. I don't know, but clam up he did.

Even though his silence made me uncomfortable, I didn't stop. Scared or not, I had to get through it. I didn't believe I was going to get any better opportunity, so I just plowed on. I told Moore how I had applied several months earlier for a teaching position but had received no response from the district. As I spoke, his face began to drain of its baby-pink hue into an unhealthy, almost predeath chalkiness. This noticeable change in color was coupled with Mr. Moore slowly crumpling lower in his chair. His silhouette began to take on a disconcerting blob-like shape.

I was suddenly struck with the thought that I was clearly unnerving him—how strange. As I was trying to sort out in my mind why he was continually rearranging three or four pens on his desk, I realized he was probably more scared of me than I was of him. This stunning conclusion caused me to take my level of confrontation down a tad. I was very well acquainted with how it felt to respond from guilt, and he was demonstrating all the characteristics of guilt-ridden responses.

It appeared Harold, as I now began to fondly think of him, was feeling as though he were in over his head. If he was a secret member of the Klan, as I often assumed most unknown white men were since Ned's arrest, he had clearly missed the Klan training sessions on basic bullying.

Then Harold began to hem and haw with sounds that made no literal sense—just high-pitched squeakiness. I really didn't know how to respond to his noises, so I just trekked on, plunking my folder of personal papers carefully on top of the piles of paperwork on his desk. I slowly untied the string around the folder, and with a slight dramatic flair, I pulled out the copies I had placed inside. I went through each document one by one to build my case. Then I said to Harold, "I am aware of the fact that people with less education, little or no teaching experience, and even lacking teaching credentials have been hired by the Mobile County school district—after I applied."

I concluded, "Mr. Moore, can you tell me that the last person you hired as a teacher in either of my two credentialed areas was more qualified than I am?"

Well, once again poor Harold resorted to silence. In growing nervousness, I said to him with all the outrageous Southern charm I could gather, "I am considering filing a civil rights lawsuit against the district citing discrimination in hiring based on my husband's activity in the civil rights movement." Grasping tightly to the arm of the chair to steady my nerves, I took a deep breath and continued with as much artificial sweetness as I could muster. "Mr. Moore, you really must give me an explanation as to the district's refusal to hire me. I am sure you can understand my unhappiness, being the gentleman that you are. You see, Mr. Moore, I just want to teach in the Mobile public schools."

Silence filled the office for what seemed to be an eternity. Then Harold gathered all his pens together into one tight fist and noisily cleared his throat with a sound that might have come from a decrepit truck motor valiantly turning over. He started to speak, but the words that came out at first just didn't make sense: "Yes . . . aha, the . . . I mean . . . ah, OK . . ." I was at a complete loss as to what to do next. With my hands discreetly folded in my lap, I just sat smiling quietly like how I thought a "little lady" would.

Finally, Harold pulled himself up straighter in his chair and thrust his fist full of pens purposefully in the direction of the outer office. He called out loudly, "Miss Brogan, bring me an application for a teaching position." Well, there you were. Harold Moore had asked me to sit and complete the application right in front of him because he said that he himself planned to follow its progress step by step. Once he started talking, he couldn't seem to stop. But in all of his long string of words and giggle-like sounds, he made no comment as to what had happened to my last application. I had the distinct feeling, though, that this application was going to receive more attention than the last one had. I asked how long it would take for a response from the district, and he assured this "little lady," as he continued to call me, that it shouldn't take long at all.

Handing him the finished application, I stood slowly, trying to take in what had just happened. Harold thrust out his hand over the desk, and I felt his soft, flabby hand in mine shaking it with great vigor. Overcome with happy feelings, I began to think that maybe I should have hugged poor Harold in addition to the handshake. Outside of Miss Brogan's office, my feet carried me quickly back to my car.

During the drive back to work, the poignant civil rights mantra played nonstop in my head:

> We shall overcome, we shall overcome
> We shall overcome some day.
> Oh, deep in my heart, I do believe
> We shall overcome some day.

I thought to myself that maybe, just maybe, there really was some truth to those intoxicating words. Then I remembered how it felt as a child after a day in the sun playing on the beach, my shoulders bright red with sunburn. My mother would soothe the burning by gently patting on cool vinegar. Could it be the words of this powerful prayer were bringing cool vinegar relief to my anxiety?

And true to his word, a letter arrived in my mailbox three days later offering me a teaching position with the Mobile County public schools. The letter stated that the district was offering me a special-education teacher position at St. Elmo High School for the upcoming school year. Looking at the letter more closely, though, I understood the offer had been carefully crafted to discourage me from accepting the job.

The letter said the job would be in Bayou La Batre, the small shrimp-fishing village located in the southern end of Mobile County on the Gulf Coast—several miles from my home in suburban Mobile. Without a doubt, the assignment would potentially put me at risk of Klan violence again on lonely roads as I traveled long distances back and forth to work.

Next, the teaching credentials I held specified the subject areas I was qualified to teach: English and history. The special-education teaching offer was unexplainable. Although I held valid teaching credentials for English and history, I did not have a credential to cover special education.

And lastly, in the 1968–69 school year, St. Elmo High School was still an exclusively segregated, entirely black school, including staff. I would be the only white person in the school.

It appeared the Mobile County school district hoped I might not accept the job offer for any one or all of those reasons. Each part of the offer had clearly been weighed to discourage me. It seemed the district held on to the hope that the deal might fall apart because of my unwillingness to accept the offer, thereby avoiding the costly and embarrassing possibility of a lawsuit.

It seemed no coincidence that my neighbor, Charlie Drum, was the Principal of St. Elmo High School—the school to which I had been assigned. So I decided Drum was the person I needed to talk to about all this. That evening, with the letter in hand, I went down the street to his house.

First, we talked about the fact that I lacked a credential in special education. I told him about my work experience in other school districts, and Charlie seemed firm in his belief that I was unofficially qualified to do a credible job teaching special education at his school. He and I agreed that if the Mobile County school district wanted to risk potential penalties from the state associated with hiring someone to teach outside what was designated on their credentials, it was nothing to us. Charlie even indicated he was aware that this kind of misassignment often occurred. So this part of the job offer was acceptable to me.

Next, Charlie told me St. Elmo High School was one of only two nonintegrated, all-black high schools in the district. He wondered how I felt about this. Charlie said he thought the district believed this fact alone would keep me from accepting the job offer—that I would be the only white person working in an all-black school. I told Charlie that from kindergarten on, I had attended schools with a rich racial mix. Now as an adult, I most willingly and happily lived in an all-black community, and socially, I moved in circles that were pretty much made up of only black friends. It seemed very odd to me that the district might think this assignment would be unacceptable because of the racial makeup of the school. In reality, that part of the offer could not have been any more to my liking. I assured Charlie I found myself eternally grateful for being welcomed into the black community. And as far as I was concerned, working in an all-black school would be heaven for me. I should be so lucky.

A final stroke of good fortune as far as the job offer was concerned came when, during the conversation, I told Charlie about my apprehension of driving alone on back country roads because of Klan threats. At that, Charlie smiled and generously offered me a place in the neighborhood car pool that traveled over thirty miles each day back and forth to St. Elmo High School. This meant I would not be commuting on the road alone anymore. And I could think of no better reason to accept the job offer than that reason alone.

A huge sense of relief rolled over me as, one by one, the potential negative parts of the job offer fell into place. I was thrilled, thinking to myself that that must have been what it felt like to float through rough waters in an inner tube of audacious grace.

I quickly called Harold Moore's office and accepted the job offer. Harold seemed a little flustered on the phone, but he acknowledged my acceptance of the teaching contract. Celebrating my victory, I turned in my notice with the welfare department, effective the last day of August. This worked out perfectly because the new job with the school district started around the first of September.

CHAPTER TWENTY

Tallulah

A dog was at the top of my "wish list" when we moved to Mobile, and I especially liked the idea of a Dalmatian. At the age of four, I'd asked Santa for a puppy, and I was delighted to receive my Christmas request a few days later. A dog has been a constant in my life ever since. The strong memory of how it felt to stand in my grandparent's wonderful kitchen on that Christmas morning holding that wiggly little creature tight in my small arms still touches a tender place in my heart. I think I knew, even at that young age, that I would never want to go long without a dog as an integral part of my life.

My grandpa and grandma Miller were, without question, major providers of happiness in my childhood. Grandpa's life as a well-respected farmer in Wellington, Ohio, long before I was born, was always the source of wonderful stories that fascinated his four granddaughters again and again. By the time I came along, the farm was long gone, but his endearing tales lingered on.

One of my favorites was the story about a dearly loved Dalmatian named Belle. As Grandpa rode his iconic chestnut horse, Lucky, proudly to open the activities of the Lorain County

Fair held each August in Wellington, Belle would run gracefully along next to Lucky, adding a touch of refined country elegance to the splendid, almost movie-star image my grandfather must have created. Sitting astride the horse, his six-foot-three frame adorned in a stylish belted tweed jacket and trousers, soft leather gloves, and Panama hat, he must have cut quite a memorable figure for the prosperous Wellington farm community in the middle of the roaring twenties. Growing up in northern Ohio close to the old farm, I would often envision Grandpa in my mind's eye, on his beautiful horse with his devoted Belle at his side. The romantic idea of a Dalmatian of my own never really left my heart.

After arriving in Mobile, I knew we could at last acquire a dog now that we had our own place, even though it was a parsonage. I was thrilled at the prospect. So the hunt was on for a Dalmatian. To my delight, an ad in a small local Mobile newspaper offered a Dalmatian puppy for sale at a farm outside of town. With great excitement, Ned and I set off to check out the dog. My heart was pounding quickly as Ned pulled our car into the red dirt drive of the shabby-looking pecan farm. The farmer, dressed in loose, bib-front farm overalls topped off with a huge brimmed sun hat, languidly led Ned and me into a dilapidated barn behind the house. And there, lying on the red dirt in a boxed-off corner of a horse stall, I saw an adorable little white dog with small, round black spots splattered over her wiggling body. As I picked her up and held her close, her warm little pink tongue lovingly licked my hand. And at that moment, I knew my dream of owning my own Dalmatian had come true.

Ned was almost as excited as I was over our new acquisition. And as new pet owners, it didn't take long for us to discover some interesting characteristics of our active puppy. For example, no one had told us that the breed had been developed in Europe to provide escort for horse-drawn coaches on long trips between villages. Perhaps with Dalmatians racing close to the horses' hoofs, other dogs along the road would be bullied away from frightening the horses. Also, the common vision that we have in our heads today of Dalmatians sitting on the front seat of fire engines is a misleading notion. Unlike the popular myth, these dogs do not see themselves as decorative fixtures. Dalmatian DNA is infused with incredible endurance. These dogs basically need daily exercise involving some rigorous activity. Playing the role of a quiet, staid house pet, or decorative accessory to a service vehicle, does not really fit their inner life purpose very well, as we were to quickly find out.

My mother suggested a name for our puppy that had connections to Alabama folk history. Years earlier, Tallulah Bankhead, the daughter of a nationally known Alabama politician, had been a famous actress. And since she had been active in liberal causes despite her Southern roots, it seemed appropriate to my mother that we grace our Dalmatian with the rather exotic-sounding name Tallulah. And we agreed.

In Tallulah's first two years, we were living in the parsonage on Merritt Drive. And even with our best efforts, by the time she was a year old, we had pretty much given up attempting to confine her to the yard for any period of time when we weren't home.

At first, we tried a large, screw-in yard device that had a light-weight chain attached. But the screw-in chain, impaled securely in the soil of the backyard, actually became an embarrassing disaster. Before we left the house, we would attach Tallulah to the end of the chain, which could spin in a circle, giving her plenty of room to maneuver all around the yard. It also allowed for space to enter her doghouse situated beneath the shade of a large tree. We left out many of her favorite chew toys and tons of water. We ignorantly believed we had humanely confined our sweet dog.

But according to a watchful neighbor, despite our best planning, after we would drive away, our muscular dog would almost effortlessly pull out the screw-in chain from the yard and proceed to drag it behind her on a happy jaunt through our neighbors' yards. A little later in the day when one of us would come home to check on her, Tallulah would not be in our backyard at all. She would excitedly welcome us at the front door, easily dragging the chain and attached screw-in thing behind her. Entangled with flowers and other related landscape trophies, the apparatus became a way for her to bring home beautiful presents from her delighted wanderings. To be clear, the neighbors were not at all happy with our faulty method of confining our trusted pet.

When these confinement attempts proved unworkable, we turned to plan B—leaving her alone inside the parsonage. Not being shy, our zealous Dalmatian found several objects to occupy her interest inside the house. One project she took on demonstrated her architectural design skill. She would carefully chew off the bottom corners of each of the lower kitchen cabinet doors. Each door then became more rounded off where previously a square corner had been. The result certainly gave the kitchen a down-home, rustic look, although I don't think the church parishioners, who were considered the owners of the residence, saw this as an improvement.

But without question, Tallulah's favorite way to spend her daytime hours was playing with expensive textbooks and other large, treasured theology volumes Ned had acquired during his seminary years. She irreverently shredded these tomes one bite at a time. Book spines were her favorite delicacy. And when we got home, she would be leaping about in the mess of what was left of the books for that day, roaring to go out and run her legs off. The special glue in the spine of the larger books must have provided exceptional fuel for her limitless energy.

The year was 1966, in semirural Alabama. Please remember, times were different, and attitudes toward responsible pet ownership were different. I hope you don't think me too disgustingly irresponsible as a pet parent, but out of frustration, we finally decided to just let Tallulah go out on her own and run loose during the day. The church council was unwilling to fence the large yard for us, and we didn't have the resources to do so ourselves. So this was our final resort, since all our other plans had ended badly.

And just as we thought we had resolved our issues with Tallulah, we learned otherwise. When the open-door policy began, we witnessed as our dog's happy daily jaunts turned into amazing adventures. After letting her loose and being away for a while, we would arrive home to find her joyfully welcoming us at our front door. Next to her would be an assorted collection of leather sports items—sometimes baseballs, sometimes baseball gloves, sometimes catcher's mitts, and once even a football. We didn't live near any park or schoolyard. Further complicating this disconcerting picture, of course, was the fact that we didn't even have children upon which to surreptitiously pin this pile of loot.

The big question for us was: How did the stuff get there? It would seem that Tallulah, in her diverse travels, had apparently found where children engaged in sports activities. She then must have waited close by for these various leather sports items to be left untouched for just a moment or so. Then, quick like lightning, she had to have snatched the thing up, racing home to our front door with the delicious prize in her mouth. After depositing the sports gear at our front entryway, she would go off again to find another wonderful gift for us. In retrospect, as we considered her amazing collection, we believe the football must have been the challenge of the year for her to get home. I would have tried to return the pilfered items if I had any idea where or from whom she had snatched them, but I didn't have a clue.

Even four-plus decades later, while I was cleaning out a closet just the other day, I found what I think was probably the last of Tallulah's cherished catcher's mitt trophies. I am happy to say it ended up going out the door with my eighteen-year-old grandson after he inspected it and pronounced it "really old." It would appear he perceived it as a treasured bit of antiquity. And to me, it surely was. I can't think of any better place it should now be destined to live than with him. And best of all, the surprising find warmed my heart with another wonderful memory of my indomitable Tallulah Dalmatian.

After Ned's arrest and our secret move in the night away from the parsonage to our new home into the heart of the black community, our devoted Dalmatian was happier than ever. Immediately after the move, we installed a tall bamboo fence behind our newly rented house to try another round of containment. But she showed us right away that neither our new fence, nor the six-foot-high school yard fence all along the back of our property, would stop her from escaping. We finally learned, unequivocally, that no normal fence would confine our agile dog.

Once again, we were given a choice—to allow Tallulah to run loose during the day or to confine her inside the house. I am not proud to say this, but out of frustration, we chose the open-door option yet again. Very soon, Tallulah discovered a couple of carefree neighborhood dog friends to pal around with, and so began the next chapter in the life of our superhero Dalmatian. Each day, paired up with her new friends, another adventure would present itself.

The kitchen of our new place faced the front of the house with almost floor-to-ceiling windows. The bottom row of windows could be opened out a little way to let in some coastal breezes when the wind was right. So before I left for school each day, Tallulah's two new buddies, George (named for the racist Alabama Governor George Wallace, known far and wide for his hate-filled rhetoric), and Rap (named for the famous black activist, Rap Brown), would show up sniffing noisily at the partially opened kitchen windows to call for Tallulah. These resolute creatures, beloved members of the black community we lived in, had been given names that would not have been tolerated in the white communities of Mobile. The silly irony was that, although George Wallace was a white man, George, the dog, was a large blackish-brown animal with steely black eyes and semi-shaggy, tangled hair. And although Rap Brown was a proud, impeccably groomed black man, Rap, the dog, was a good-size, creamy-white but perpetually dirty creature with haunting gray eyes and soft scruffy hair. Each day, this unlikely pair named after a would-be civil rights hero and a first-class racist would appear at about the same time, waiting with excited anticipation at my front kitchen window to be joined by our black-and-white movie actress/activist Dalmatian.

When I opened the kitchen door, our Tally, as she became fondly known to us, would joyfully run out to join her two faithful friends. And none of the three would care a whit what their names or their appearances meant to anyone as long as they could run free together for a while each day. Not to put too fine a point on it, but George and Rap were clearly good moral influences on our dog. Our disreputable Dalmatian appeared to stop her thieving ways while she was out and about with her two new buddies. And for that we were grateful. She would arrive home each day, sans leather gifts for us, but delightfully worn out from her day's activities with George and Rap. The trade-off suited us just fine.

The place Tallulah held in my life was crucial to my healthy emotional balance. Pretty much from the beginning, I perceived my marriage in clear terms. Ned was completely obsessed with his righteous calling as a minister. It was his reason for existing. With great ferociousness, he centered on being a man of God who promoted issues of justice. And to be clear, this was laudable, indeed. But in the wake of all this, I was left lonely and bereft. I felt completely unimportant to my spouse. Finding the energy to be a devoted husband rarely if ever seemed to interest Ned. His passion to "serve others"—a group that did not include me—consumed his every waking thought. For the most part, I felt like an unwanted interruption to his really important work.

But during these times of experiencing emotional abandonment, my dear Tallulah was the closest friend I had. She snuggled with me and eased my loneliness when I was morose and homesick during those first months in Mobile. Daily, I told her my deepest thoughts. I talked to her about lost dreams. I told her about what I'd thought life would be like as a new bride—adored and indulged—and about how disappointed I was that the dream hadn't materialized. She continually listened to me with extraordinary patience and attentiveness. Each night, she slept stretched across the foot of the bed. She remained faithfully at my side and licked my hand when I stood alone in the kitchen, frozen in fear, listening to the horrible Klan phone threats the night of Ned's arrest. I held nothing back with her. Her loving presence always, always consoled me. In honest truthfulness, I don't really know how I would have survived without her.

Then in 1969, as life moved on, we found ourselves living again in northern Ohio. After our last year in Mobile, except for occasional family visits to my parents' apple farm, Tallulah never again had the opportunity to run free. My savvy dog learned how to contend with sharp, cool breezes and brilliantly colored leaves that flitted rudely about in the small yard of our new home in East Cleveland. Eventually, she mastered the downright bitter cold winter winds blowing in off Lake Erie, which brought smothering mounds of frigid snow. I'm certain all this was a shock to her warm, Southern Alabama spirit.

And as the family expanded, she responded with gentle love toward our new little daughter. Almost daily, Tallulah and I took long walks with Megan in the stroller. My nimble dog was always the perfect escort—just like good Dalmatians know how to be—trotting loyally next to the wheels of the carriage. It is safe to say that my sweet friend never lost her joyful spirit outdoors, and she ultimately became quite content lying in front of our warm fireplace during the winter months.

Seven years later, we ended up in Los Angeles, California, the last home of her namesake, Tallulah Bankhead. My sweet dog dropped over one sunny afternoon in the living room of our California parsonage. We quickly rushed her off to an animal hospital, where we lost her shortly after our arrival. Because we wanted to know what had caused her death, we had an autopsy done, apparently not an unusual practice when pets seem to go quickly in non-trauma-related cases. She had diabetes. We didn't know this was a possibility for a dog. The autopsy also showed she had BBs embedded in her back, something else we weren't aware of—probably from her days of proudly dragging home leather sports trophies for us. It surely doesn't take much imagination to picture an irate young boy standing with a BB gun aimed at the thief of his valued baseball glove as she ran wildly away from him with the treasure in her mouth.

The loss of Tallulah in 1978 sorely wrenched my heart. My endearing Dalmatian was my primary emotional support during the most tumultuous years of my life. I am forever grateful to her, and I will never forget the sustaining love she brought me when I needed it most.

CHAPTER TWENTY-ONE

St. Elmo Odyssey

According to the 1960 census, the shrimp-fishing village of Bayou La Batre was about 80 percent white. St. Elmo was the segregated black high school for children of the remaining 20 percent or so of the residents of Bayou La Batre and the surrounding communities. The day I started working at St. Elmo, I was the only white person at the school—student or staff.

Because few, if any, black families had the financial resources to be a part of the shrimp-fishing industry, families of St. Elmo High School students were totally dependent on marginal custodial jobs, day housecleaning work, and occasional handyman situations. This work was almost always only part-time and required strong backs and a willingness to do anything unpleasant that white workers did not want to do—for pittance pay. Families in the St. Elmo area scrambled simply to put food on the table, and education, although valued, was not actually seen as a way out of the economic dead end in which they lived.

The morning of the staff meeting before the beginning of the school year at St. Elmo High School, I stepped into Charlie Drum's car with three other neighborhood women, who were also teachers at the school. I was excited to be starting another teaching job, and as Charlie backed out of the driveway, I chattered along, giggling. The car-pool group was a kick, and immediately I felt right at home with them, and especially with Clemmie Reed, the history and government teacher. The best part was that I no longer had to make scary trips alone in my car nervously watching out for trashy pickup trucks with Confederate flags and overloaded gun racks. What a relief.

Meeting the St. Elmo staff was fun. Clemmie adopted me, shepherding me around and introducing me to people. I felt welcome right from the start. I understood that I had some special worth to them because of my relationship with that much-talked-about white man who had stunned the community with his courageous actions in the Prichard arrest saga. Charlie Drum had referenced my relationship to Ned in passing when he'd introduced me, and the endearing smiles and great kindness I saw in my colleagues' eyes assured me of an honest feeling of acceptance.

Clemmie sat herself down next to me, quietly giving me insider information on who taught what, and whom I should get to know because of special school jobs they held—like Shorty John, who taught PE and math but who was also responsible for checking buses in and out each day. He was a good person to know if I had to find missing students first thing in the morning.

I just felt a little uncomfortable tagging along on Ned's coattails, though. I wanted to think I was making it on my own. Life was becoming something of a challenge living as an appendage to someone with Ned's celebrity. The position had some lovely advantages, like the Sunday-morning church experiences, the neat neighborhood connections, and, without question, the opportunity to teach again, which had come from Ned's prominence. But I didn't find much satisfaction in always being in Ned's shadow, either. I hoped my teaching job would give me the opportunity to begin to emerge on my own a little.

In the afternoon after the main teacher meeting in the cafeteria was over, Charlie took me to see my classroom. The idea of teaching special education had motivated me to do a good deal of outside reading regarding instructional strategies for special-needs kids, and I was feeling more confident about the whole situation than I had a few weeks earlier.

I was eager to see the actual room where I would be working. The school had been built on a formerly marshy piece of land with really no other structures close by, just scrubby-looking vegetation. My classroom was located toward the back of the sprawling one-story building. As Charlie opened the classroom door, I saw that all the necessary features for a functional classroom were there: plenty of space, a wall of windows, a couple dozen single-student desks, a large wooden teacher desk and sturdy chair, a clean linoleum floor, and florescent lights overhead. The room even had the requisite blackboard stretching the width of the room, as well as a few chunky built-in cabinets across the back wall.

Now, all the important elements that would make it a workable classroom were there, *except* it lacked any additional critical learning resources. Maps, books, posters, an overhead projector, screens, dictionaries, and instructional wall art were nonexistent. Not even a scrap of paper sat in the built-in cabinets. It was as if the room had been cleared of everything but the very barest of essentials. This was my introduction to teaching on the margins—the fundamental fact of life for the entire facility of St. Elmo High School. The building and necessary furnishings were supplied, but any additional instructional support to inspire and enhance learning that was found in most other schools was missing.

On the first day of classes, I woke up early and fixed toast and coffee for a quick breakfast. A straight cotton shift dress I had made seemed like a good choice, paired with comfortable low-heeled shoes. The night before, I had bundled up a few teacher resource books, handouts, and pencils and pens, along with extra lined paper, Kleenex, and purse essentials, and I had put everything into a large canvas tote. Since Ned had already left, I fed Tallulah and sent her on her way when Rap and George came to the front windows. Then I grabbed the tote and practically flew out the kitchen door and down the street to Charlie's house where he and my car-pool pals were waiting in the driveway.

Arriving at school, we were encapsulated in a bubble of school busses. I don't think I had ever seen so many in one place before. Enthusiastically, I walked to my room with my tote over my shoulder, oblivious to any reactions around me. It didn't really seem like my presence should be a big deal to anyone at all. I had attended school from kindergarten through high school in classrooms that were fully integrated, so racial differences in a school were not an issue in my mind whatsoever. I walked into my classroom, deposited my stuff on the teacher's desk, and sat down to collect my thoughts. I felt great. Here I was, finally in a classroom again. What fun this was going to be—I could hardly wait.

A few minutes before the start of class, a short young man dressed in well-worn denim pants and threadbare T-shirt ambled into the room. He looked startled when he saw me, and my enthusiastic hi was not well received. His eyes focused on me for a few seconds, and then he clumsily backed out of the room without making a sound.

From the enrollment roster, I knew I had about fifteen students who were scheduled to be with me all day; at that time, the strategy of mainstreaming special-education students was not yet common. Little information had been provided to help me understand the specific disabilities of each student, but it was clear each of them had been academically unsuccessful in regular education classes over the years. The majority of the kids on the list had been together in the same special-education class for most of their school experience.

When the young man backed out of the room, I stood up and followed him to the door. Outside, three or four teenagers stood around in a shy, rather bedraggled-looking clump staring at me with large, distrustful eyes. Another six or so more students stood farther back, scattered around the edges of the hallway. All were looking at me with immense caution. It would seem no one had warned them that the former teacher had left, and I was the replacement. To add to this complicated mess, not only was I the new teacher, but I was—God forbid—white.

I hadn't anticipated how my appearance might affect them. In fact, in my earth-shattering naiveté, it had never crossed my mind that racial differences would present a conflict at all. I hadn't considered the possibility that I would be seen as an unwanted outsider. In retrospect, though, it was the same dynamic that had been in play when Father Francis Walter had come upon the awesome quilts on a clothesline in Gee's Bend. He was unable to find the lady of the house to ask her about the quilts, because when the lady of the house—a rural black woman—saw a white man coming to her door she fled to the woods behind her house. She, like the rural students at St. Elmo, knew from over a century of experience that unknown white folks were not to be trusted with even so much as eye contact.

So my first challenge of the day was to try to engage my fearful students. I introduced myself and explained I was the new teacher. I said, "I really do want to get to know you. Why don't you come on into the room and sit down so we can talk." I told them I wanted to know what it was like to live in St. Elmo. I said I had so much to learn about them and about where they lived, and that they were the ones who would be teaching me all that. Two or three warmed up a little and walked slowly into the classroom. But to my surprise and frustration, the others turned and almost ran away in the other direction.

I followed the few willing kids into the room, then pulled up a student desk close to them and sat down. They continued to look at me as though I were a formidable entity, but I just tried to smile and talk as though everything were perfectly fine. The tension in the room was palpable. Then one girl about fourteen gathered her courage and spoke up loudly in a heavy rural drawl. "Miss, do ya'll have to stay here? This here is our room. Why dun-ya go away?" Well, her solution was simple: just erase me, and everything would be all right again. But as disconcerting as her sentiment sounded, the good thing was that at least now the students were talking to me.

At that moment, Charlie Drum walked into the room with the other students who had run away when I'd asked them to come into the room a few minutes before.

Charlie had a wide grin on his face, and no superhero could have done more to turn things around for me than he did. Talking to them like the reliable friend he was, he cheerfully told the discombobulated group of kids to just sit down and be quiet. I was certain Charlie had gathered up all the escapees and brought the entire missing group of special-ed kids along with him. So at least all my charges were collected in one place at the same time. That seemed a bit of a victory in and of itself.

The warm and endearing relationship between Charlie and the kids was evident. They clearly trusted him, not only as a school official but also as someone who they knew protected and looked out for them. Charlie then walked over to me and put his hand loosely on my shoulder. More powerful than words, the action resonated throughout the room. The students who struggled with verbal communication and other basic social cues understood the strong message his hand on my shoulder sent, and the room almost instantly calmed down.

Charlie told the kids I was the new teacher, and he told them that if they would give me a chance, he knew they would start to like me. Then the floodgates opened. Students slid back into their seats and began to call out, "Who is she?" Then: "Mr. Drum, she's a foreigner. She talks too fast!" And with great emphasis: "We can't understand her."

Charlie took the time to tell the class that the teacher from last year had taken another job and wasn't coming back. He stated clearly, "Mrs. Milner is my choice of a fine teacher for this class." He said he expected them to show respect and welcome me. He also said that he wanted them to cooperate and do what I asked them to do. By the time he left, the open hostility in the room had been replaced by a neutral truce. I was delighted.

I was certainly confused, though. Again, my cultural ignorance had taken the day, as I had never considered that my white skin or the way I spoke would be disadvantages in being a successful teacher at St. Elmo. At that time in my life, the concept of "white privilege," or seeing my white way of relating to the world as really the acceptable standard for everyone, had not come full circle in my brain. But when my way of communicating with the world was challenged by these awesome teenagers, and when my skin color was seen as a detriment, not the proper standard, I had to do some serious reassessing.

Without a doubt, I wanted to be effective in my new teaching job, so I knew that meant I was going to have to make some significant changes. I couldn't change the color of my skin, but I could slow down my speech a bit. And I could try to take the edge off my Northern accent. In fact, after a little practice, I found that if I tried hard enough, I could almost speak in a soft, slow drawl myself. The sense that I was an unacceptable outsider because of my white skin, though, took much more time to overcome.

I was happy that nothing had been said about Ned and his arrest to the students. I didn't really want that baggage thrown into the drama, because I saw this as my chance to do well at what I liked to do best—teach. I considered this new and challenging social environment a gift. I believed the St. Elmo experience was going to be a measure of my worth, not anyone else's. I wanted to interact and teach from *my* frame of reference—not my husband's.

Attitudes began to mellow after the opening-day drama was over. Kids began softly telling me their names, and then they shared with me a little about what class had been like before I'd come. I found this exceedingly valuable, as I wanted to keep the rituals and schedule as close to their comfort level as I could, at least at the beginning.

As time went by, Pauline, the first girl who had spoken up and had asked me to leave, stepped up and took a prominent place in the class. She assumed the unofficial role of leader, and she felt she should keep me informed as to how things should be done.

Looking for any cooperation I could get, I began to rely on Pauline. In response, she came out of her crusty, defensive shell very fast. It didn't take long for me to realize that she found great satisfaction in telling others what they should be doing, and when they should be doing it. For example, any time the class was expected to line up for some activity or other, Pauline would staunchly plant her wide feet, which were covered in floppy, paper-thin leather shoes, and move the top half of her solid, five-foot-one frame in dramatic sweeping actions, thereby signaling she had taken charge. Then she would pull impressively at the short sprigs of tight black braids arrayed around her head and direct the lining-up process by calling out names and instructing each classmate as to where they were to stand in the line. Finally, she would resort to physically rearranging kids who were moving too slow for her liking. The chemise-like outfits she often wore, made from recycled flour sacks, only seemed to add a sense of populist energy to her behavior, which tested my patience a bit. Her dark eyes always flashed when she felt herself "in charge," just as they had when she'd told me I should go away. And to be clear, at those moments, every living creature in the classroom took notice. I didn't always respond to Pauline's stubbornness in textbook teacher fashion. I was, at times, rather short-tempered with her, but my clumsy efforts in dealing with Pauline did teach me a whole lot about forbearance.

Another student, Antowan, was usually open to new ideas. He carried a sense of enthusiasm for life, being one of the kids who had initially played escape artist. But once he'd settled into the classroom, Antowan began to open up and talk a good deal. As time went on, I saw him as a surprisingly savvy, fairly articulate kid who wanted to be seen as Mr. Helpful. At fifteen years old, and about five foot five, he was the class charmer, with a sunny smile that demonstrated his need to be the center of attention. His actions were quick, and he never liked to sit still for long, always moving his lanky legs with agility. Antowan was, sadly, the only student I saw as having possible promise of a productive future in the world on his own. His academic skills were limited, but his ability to problem solve was quite good. He occasionally wore clothes that were less countrified and rural and more city teenager than any of the others, which made me wonder how he had that advantage. How did he sometimes acquire the more up-to-date, store-bought clothing? But this is only one of the carload of mysteries that still plague my memories from that classroom.

Daily, kids showed up wearing makeshift or leftover clothes. But the real challenge for families was footwear, obviously the most difficult item to find. The shoes the kids showed up wearing really didn't come close to fitting their feet at all.

The class had many academic shortcomings, as well: not one student in my class of fifteen or so teenagers had reading skills beyond a second-grade level, and their math skills were extraordinarily limited. Additionally, each student had lingering deficits in basic social skills.

Every day, I felt like the academic and social wounds were gaping holes, and all I could do was try to put mini bandages over the gaps. Sometimes it seemed like a small bandage would stick for a while, but then other days even the tiniest of bandages wouldn't stay on for a moment.

I just kept feeling that somehow life was going to get better for these kids who had been given such heavy baggage to carry. They each entered the classroom every day with such extraordinary dignity. And these beautiful children who had been temporarily loaned to me were so willing to try whatever was asked of them time after time. There was no way I was giving up on them. That would have been as though I were giving up on myself. So I just kept plodding along, taking it one day at a time.

CHAPTER TWENTY-TWO

Tiny Silk Ribbons

Plodding around in jean shorts and a T-shirt one lazy Saturday morning, I found myself fixing breakfast in my sunny kitchen. Tallulah was impatiently sitting next to the low, half-open window waiting for her buddies, Rap and George. I leaned over to give her a loving pat and was sucked into her enthusiastic response. It wasn't hard to see that she was happily devoted to the latest daily adventures with her two roustabout doggie pals. With her tail wildly wagging, her irrepressible excitement was contagious. All this fierce abandon made me feel like surely something good was in the air. After living a couple of months hunkered down in our new community, and happily teaching at St. Elmo High School, I found myself feeling more calm and certainly more secure than I had for a long time after Ned's arrest.

Yet, under everything, angry feelings continued roiling inside me. Even the act of fixing a simple breakfast in my own home on a quiet Saturday morning carried an undertone of apprehension. Who knew when a car filled with white supremacists would drive by and someone would shoot at us, or when we would find an ugly burning cross terrorizing us on our front lawn some awful evening? My hostility toward Ned for putting me in this situation of continual under-the-radar fear hadn't lessened. It was always there, sticking relentlessly to my simple, everyday existence. I just couldn't get past the notion that my husband—the one person in my life who was supposed to take care of me, protect me, and honor me—was the very person who had put me out there with a Ku Klux Klan bull's-eye on my back. He had never even asked me, *Are you OK with my decision to get arrested?* The destructive force of what I perceived to be Ned's betrayal was seriously fracturing our marriage.

Every day, the poison ate a little deeper into my soul. Ned and I didn't make any effort to try to heal the damage. I guess we weren't really up to the task of figuring out how to do that. Ned wouldn't discuss anything to do with the arrest, and I didn't challenge him. Despite feeling betrayed, I believed I had to make the best of the situation for the sake of our marriage. That's what a good wife was supposed to do, wasn't it? Just getting through each day as best we could without saying much to each other, especially regarding the arrest, seemed to be the only way to live our lives as man and wife. We danced around the toxic issue as if it didn't exist by pretending everything was somehow all right. I survived in my little world—held together by a thin layer of rubbery guilt stretched wide to cover my un-wifely feelings of bitterness toward Ned.

I was surviving in the world of "let's pretend everything's all right" that Saturday morning when I heard a knock at the kitchen door. Looking through the window, I saw my next-door neighbor, Amelia Walker. The Walkers were great neighbors—always looking for ways to help us out. The kids did yard work for us, and Amelia often brought over home-cooked meals. They were kind and generous in their efforts to help us feel welcome.

Standing next to Amelia was a small, ebony-hued, elderly woman, arm in arm with her. I had never seen her before. I didn't know that a few days earlier Amelia had asked Ned if she could bring her mother by to meet him. Now here they were. When I opened the door, I sensed an unexplainable aura of dignity surrounding the women standing in front of me. But even to this day, I almost always feel this remarkable energy when I am around black women. I'm not sure exactly why. But I do not doubt my intuition about this whatsoever. And this energy—saturated with unabashed warmth, strength, wisdom, and good humor—cannot help but draw me in whenever I am fortunate enough to connect with it.

With a wide smile, Amelia introduced me to her mother. Elizabeth Homer was wearing an immaculate dress that had clearly been a companion of hers for years. It looked as though the lacey white collar softly surrounding her neck might have been recently added to freshen things up. Heavy pinkish-gray stockings hung in geometric wrinkles circling her knees and ankles, and on her feet were well-worn dressy black shoes. Looking into Elizabeth's eyes, I read a hint of uneasiness. Her mouth, pulled into a tight line, was turned up only slightly at each corner.

Amelia said her mother was visiting from her home "up in Lowndes County." Elizabeth Homer's silver-gray hair, carefully rolled into small sausages, was then pinned into place around the back of her head. Responding to my smile, I saw bright rays of sunlight sparkling back at me from her dark eyes. Completely taken in by the fortitude found in her deeply lined face, I invited the women in, delighted with the prospect of company.

The two women walked slowly, almost as one, into the middle of the kitchen. Amelia pulled herself up and tightened the hold she had on her mother's arm, as though empowering her with strength. And Elizabeth held tighter and tighter to her daughter's hand while allowing a lovely half smile to begin to unfold on her face. The whole scene seemed a bit odd—a bit strained. This, apparently, was something more than just a nice neighborly visit, and I had no clue what was about to happen.

Then, as if on cue, Ned walked in, framed by the kitchen door. When Amelia saw Ned, her face lit up like a Christmas tree. She and her mother exchanged excited glances. The nervousness in Elizabeth's face melted into wide-eyed admiration as she looked at my husband—the man who was the source of my stuffed-away resentment.

Sometimes a word or a string of words imprint themselves on my heart for all time—words spoken in a mind-numbing instant like "Here is your new grandson" or "I love you, will you marry me?" These moments tuck themselves into my memory bag, each attached to a thin, pastel-colored silk ribbon. The grace-encrusted ribbon makes for easy retrieval of this memory whenever I might need it. The soft-spoken words from the extraordinary black woman standing in front of me still remain, even decades later, tucked away, with a fragile silk ribbon attached, in this same memory bag.

"My mama takes the long trip on dat nasty ol' bus from Lowndes County all da way down here to Mobile for jus' one reason. I writes her a letter and tells her that the Reverend Mil-lin-er, dat white man everybody talkin' bout, move right into the house next to me—yes, right next to me!" Amelia stops for a moment in her speech to add a *yes sirree* kind of gleeful laugh. Then she goes on: "My mama tol' me she gunna come to Mobile and see dat man for herself before she die—and Lordy, here she be."

At that Elizabeth Homer broke out into a smile that seemed to engulf her whole body. Her small feet moved about quickly in an excited little dance. Amelia continued, "She want to see for herself dat white man who say what he say and do what he do for our peoples. She never think she gunna ever see no white man like him—ever."

Elizabeth Homer had grown up in a culture of unbelievably poor sharecroppers. Her parents had been born slaves in the rural south-central Alabama area known as "Bloody Lowndes"— bloody for the cruel history of race-based violence toward African American citizens. Her long life had been a harsh struggle for basic survival. And here was this phenomenal soul—standing in my kitchen brimming with humble appreciation for my husband—my unfeeling, inconsiderate bastard of a husband. Incredulous, I could do nothing more than just stand there emotionally frozen.

Amelia then formally introduced her mother to Ned. He stood still for a moment taking in the import of her words. Then he stepped forward, enfolding Elizabeth's small wrinkled hands in both of his. Next, in what was for him an unusual act, he gently wrapped his arms around Elizabeth's tiny frame, gathering the sweet spirit up and holding her close as he moved slowly in half circles. Processing Amelia's words had brought a look of great satisfaction to my husband as he soaked up Elizabeth's warm admiration.

For me, time stood still. The look of sheer delight on Elizabeth's face as she was caught up in Ned's arms spoke volumes to my heart. And at that very second, the bubbling pot of animosity within began to drain away. This encounter with these two women became the very essence of grace—the instant when healing replaced anger inside me.

Never before had I experienced a reality that jolted my sensibilities as this had. Gratitude filled the now-empty space inside me where fury and trepidation had found such a comfy nesting place. It was surprisingly clear now why everything had happened as it had. Although it would take a while to try to refit many of the broken pieces back into our marriage, the healing process had surely been started by the beautiful smile on Elizabeth's face.

The magic of the moment, however, was lost in the noisy arrival of Rap and George, Tallulah's doggie friends. Running my hand over my check to wipe away tears, I opened the outside door, freeing my delighted dog to go on her merry way for the day with her buddies.

Thinking about the experience later, I understood how blessed I was to have had this extraordinary human being teach me about forgiveness—forgiveness of Ned, yes—but also forgiveness of myself, all wrapped in the same package. It came to me that by forgiving my determined husband, I was also forgiving myself of my rage toward him. And even more deeply, I was freeing myself of the guilt that came as a by-product of that rage.

All this felt really, really good. I finally "got it." What my committed spouse had done on impulse when facing arrest, and then when speaking truth to power with a journalist on that hot afternoon in June—wasn't about me at all. He'd had to do it. Every fiber in his being had demanded he be true to himself. I could no longer pass judgment on that—as much as I seemed to have found some selfish pleasure in doing so. Ned had had to communicate his understanding of justice by his actions and words to anyone who might listen. And in the black community, at least, there were listeners aplenty who connected to his message. And so I was left only with feelings of deep and abiding pride in my courageous husband's steadfastness.

CHAPTER TWENTY-THREE

Alligator Hunts

Because there was absolutely no funding at St. Elmo High School for educational materials or instructional equipment, I brought pencils and paper from home, along with any inexpensive learning resources that I could scratch up. Chalk and blackboards were about all the school could provide. I had taught in public schools in Ohio and Illinois and had not encountered anything quite so dire as this before. The lack of resources was school-wide, not just in my classroom. But there was a silver lining to this situation, because these circumstances pushed me into some unconventional strategies, ones I really would never have considered in my past teaching jobs.

One of these unconventional strategies became known as the alligator hunt. Now there I was, a northern Ohio woman who had never even seen an alligator in a zoo, much less in the wild. But when I overheard two of my students, Antowan and Samuel, talking one day about a big "gator" they had seen down the road recently, just out taking a walk, my curiosity was piqued. It seemed to me this kind of scene might spark a few classroom conversation opportunities to help develop much-needed skills. I asked Charlie

Drum if field trips off school grounds were allowed, and he said sure. So I began our weekly neighborhood walks that became known as "alligator hunts."

The activity started by asking each student to tell me what they knew about alligators—what they looked like and where we might find them within walking distance of the school. To my surprise, the questions brought out a few interesting stories of alligator experiences from some of even the most withdrawn of students. It was a hot topic, to say the least, and prompted much-needed student interaction.

I was extremely pleased not to hear any accounts of alligator attacks on people or, even worse, of alligators eating anyone in these stories, so I trustingly felt that I was on fairly safe ground. I just paddled along once again in my overwhelming naiveté, a default frame of mind for my many months at St. Elmo. I told the kids that I thought this idea of an alligator hunt would be a good chance for them to be my teacher. I needed them to give me specific information about nearby "gators."

There was almost unanimous excitement over the prospect of an alligator hunt, except for my one dependably outspoken student, Pauline. As could have been predicted, she took a no-nonsense stance and, at first, flatly refused to participate. Staunchly planting her sturdy feet about fifteen inches apart directly in front of me with her arms tightly crossed over her chest and a look of fierce determination on her face, she adamantly declared, "No! I ain't gunna do no walk to see no gator mess!" I could always count on Pauline to question anything new with a strong sense of outrage. So I arranged an alternative placement for her the first time we went on a hunt.

Pauline stayed with my business teacher friend, Jannel, across the hall with instructions for her to complete a simple project while we were gone.

Pauline had a change of heart, though, after we returned from our first hunt. When Pauline walked into the classroom, she quickly got a picture of the excitement she had missed. The look on her face clearly spoke to the fact that she felt the time for dissension was past. That was the last time she refused to be a part of one of our alligator hunts. From then on, Pauline was an enthusiastic participant.

So this is how an alligator hunt rolled out. Before each excursion, I asked questions about what my students thought we would see and tried to encourage a response from each one. Then I would write a simplified summary version of the answers on the blackboard. Next, I would have each student do their best at copying the information from the board. Some did better than others, and some were encouraged to simply draw what they were describing to me, trying to come up with words to detail what they were seeing in their heads. Numbers generated in the conversation—like how fast alligators can move, how many we might see, and how far away we should stay from them—were used in simple math problems devised for those few who could manage math skills. So much for lack of instructional material; it appeared that alligator hunts could actually generate relevant teaching opportunities, and the whole thing was great fun in the process.

After we finished all this classroom stuff, we would take off into the hot sunshine. Heading for one of the nearby narrow sandy dirt roads that snaked along adjacent to swampy creeks, we would soon find ourselves traipsing around in layers of semitropical vegetation. The kids were good at keeping together in a fairly close group, chattering happily. Examining interesting plants, flowers, or bugs the kids wanted me to see as we walked along was an extra bonus I hadn't anticipated.

But the closer we got to the marshy areas, the more nervous I would become. Heat and humidity filled our lungs, along with strange smells of flowering plants whose names were foreign to me. Each foray was a trip into swampy, exotic-looking places I had only read about in books.

I had a deep secret, though; I was always hopeful we would never actually come upon an alligator. This whole alligator thing was really a ruse. In all my education classes and school-safety training sessions, I had never been taught the protocol for alligator encounters. So I felt way out of my element as the responsible adult in the situation. I could only hold on to the fact that not one of my students had given me any firsthand accounts of actual alligator attacks. Although, in retrospect, I probably might have expanded my research to knowledgeable adults at school, I didn't. And, to be sure, not encountering an alligator was usually the case in our weekly walks. But on at least two occasions over the period of the hunts, it turned out we did actually see alligators.

The first beast we saw, I would have missed completely had I been on my own. But I can tell you with great certainty that there really was no possibility of me ever being out there on my own. Only the top foot or so of this alligator's spiny green back was exposed in a muddy pool several yards off in the distance. He seemed to be about six feet long, and Samuel excitedly pointed him out to me. All at once, I was in a state of shock when I realized this was the real thing. But as I gathered myself together, I was grateful the beast didn't seem to notice we were even there, and thankful he never moved a smidgeon.

I stood there taking slow, deep breaths staring at the beast. Slowly, I began to feel a surprising sense of relief because, just as the kids had assured me, it appeared the alligator was just taking a morning nap in the warm water. Of course, these remarkable kids were much more comfortable seeing the animal in his home setting than I was. In order not to lose face, I struggled to compose a calm demeanor. I did not want to demonstrate any signs of fright, but down deep I had truly enormous respect for the potential ferociousness of this creature. After staring in silence for a good long time, I finally was able to spit out a few words: "Well, we have been successful. Good for us. We have actually seen what we were looking for—an alligator. Now let's go on and see what else there is around here." And so we continued our walk, giving the muddy pool a very wide berth.

But a remarkable thing had happened in this encounter. My relationship with my students had taken a surprising turn. I found myself trusting in their environmental savvy rather than them relying on my position as the all-knowing teacher—a humbling exchange of roles, to say the least. And I am sure they were as aware of this new relationship as I was.

The second alligator sighting a few weeks later was less memorable, as the beast was even farther away from us, swimming lazily down a stream in the other direction. But see him, we did. And I felt as though I had legitimately earned my webbed-feet badge as an official alligator tracker.

Back in the classroom after the hunt, each student would tell at least one thing they especially liked about the walk. The comments were written word for word on the blackboard with the name of the student giving the information. Next, the statements were combined into a class story. As a finale, one of the stronger readers, usually Antowan, would volunteer to read the story back to the class. Even though alligator hunts were probably not part of the curriculum in other schools, they gave my St. Elmo kids and me a great educational advantage, nonetheless.

My life has had recurring experiences with other, less literal, alligators. But the lessons my delightful students at St. Elmo taught me about appreciating the alligators in life have been invaluable. First, get over the fear and have fun on the journey, and second, cherish the people who are with you on the hunt. The problem is that my recollection of these lessons often fails me when I need it most.

CHAPTER TWENTY-FOUR

Faith Lutheran Church

Invitations for Ned to speak at gospel churches on Sunday mornings slowed down over time. The hyperexcitement over his arrest and related comment to the press was lessening as the weeks went by, and the list of churches willing to be seen as radical enough to invite him to speak on a Sunday morning was growing shorter.

Who knew this situation would cause another fracture in our already patched-together marriage. It happened because I felt as though I had lost my time of soul renewal each week. I had found that on a Sunday morning when Ned had no invitation to speak at a church, we just stayed home. And for me, Sunday was a challenging day to live through without experiencing church in some form or another. My entire life had centered on church attendance each Sunday. It was as natural as breathing for me. Ned and I were no longer connected to a church community since Ned had resigned from Holy Cross Lutheran Church, and I truly missed the sense of belonging that came from that relationship centered in a worship experience with the blessing of the Eucharist.

When Ned was pastor at Holy Cross, I would sometimes secretly dream of a time when he and I would sit together in a church pew during a worship service, as I believed "normal" people did. I guess this longing came from a sense of loneliness; I don't know. As shallow as it sounds, I just wanted to feel the sense that visually I belonged to someone in a church setting. I would tell myself that someday my dream would come true in some way or another.

So because we often didn't go to any church anymore on Sunday, with a sense of excitement, I asked Ned about attending church together somewhere else. A part of this eagerness came from my silly secret dream of sitting next to my husband in church. But mostly the motivation for my request was just that I wanted to experience church on Sunday.

Then a completely unexpected thing happened. My husband refused. For whatever unknown reason, he told me he didn't want to go to church. And further, he didn't want to discuss the matter, either. Trying to encourage him to change his mind was a lost cause. He flatly refused to even talk about the possibility, with no explanation for his refusal.

I learned early on in our marriage that if Ned was unwilling to discuss something, then that topic was dead. In Ned's classic demonstration of anger, his facial muscles would tighten as he angrily glared at me. Then shouting disparaging remarks and moving about with fast, strong movements, his irritation would quickly push him to stomp heavily out of the room, and usually led to him getting in the car and driving off, leaving me alone for hours at a time. I was really undone by this behavior, crying and depressed. So when signs of Ned's anger would begin, it was like a dog whistle telling me to stop doing whatever it was I was doing. My passive response was part of the unwritten, unspoken contract we shared. My part of the contract had been learned from years of attending Sunday school, church, Bible school, and prayer meetings. The lesson was simple. Do not incite your husband's anger, because good Christian wives don't provoke their husbands. And the message had been unequivocal.

Who knows what made him shut down on the church-attendance issue. But his behavior did leave me with a huge sense of disappointment. It felt as though another large, empty hole had appeared in the structure of my marriage. I was hurt and felt sorry for myself because it seemed that, once again, my presence in my husband's life was of little value to him. But to keep peace in the house, the matter was securely stuffed away in the locked box in my brain marked "Do Not Open." I wanted, after all, to be the good wife.

Even though I stopped badgering Ned about attending church with me, I was not dissuaded from doing what I needed to do. So I decided that I would go to church anyway, by myself. It really wasn't easy for me to strike out against what I saw as a strong cultural tradition—attending worship services together as man and wife. But I slowly came to the understanding that I had to trade my unhealthy attachment to tradition for the important experience of attending church. So I went alone. And I considered my best choice to be Faith Lutheran Church where Arnie was pastor. Faith was a satisfying fit for me, and after I got past all the drama of leaving the house—alone—on Sunday mornings, I began to feel right at home, just like I was supposed to be there.

Examining beliefs in my head and heart, I found I had become completely comfortable with Lutheran faith precepts, and I was absolutely sure I had evolved into a for-real Lutheran. I talked all this over with my wonderful friend and current pastor, Arnie. And in a very unorthodox step as a Lutheran pastor, Arnie did a lovely thing: he simply added my name, upon my request, to the church membership list at Faith. Usually an act of this nature would have required my attendance at information classes that prospective members were required to complete, but Arnie was gracious enough to skip that step for me. He believed I had the requisite understanding of what I was doing, and he just made membership happen. I was delighted. The extraordinary irony was that, at last I was an official member of a Lutheran church—and my husband was not the pastor. What a strange turn of fate in this remarkable journey.

So off I went, alone, each Sunday morning to worship with the members of Faith Lutheran Church. I was enormously grateful for the acceptance this congregation showed me. The worship experiences gave balance to my world and tethered my soul to a place of peace, both sorely needed commodities for me.

And once again, in a most surprising way, this whole time of painful disappointment in my life had unanticipated consequences. Because of this experience, I grew up a bit and got better in touch with a remarkable treasure—a burgeoning sense of strength as a woman who, quite astonishingly, possessed great value. I was slowly learning that I did not need to be an appendage to anyone. I was a strong, independent woman who could, in fact, take charge of her own destiny.

And to my happy surprise, Ned eventually did come around. Before too long he started attending church with me. He even officially joined the Faith Lutheran congregation as I had done. Life was improving.

CHAPTER TWENTY-FIVE

A Sanctuary

The St. Elmo teacher's lounge, a comfortable room furnished with cast-off furniture, included a two-piece sectional couch and some homey upholstered chairs—all unsoiled enough to meet my clean-freak standards but certainly showing extensive use. In the middle of the room was a large worktable with folding chairs used for paperwork and snacking. Just inside the door stood a clunky soft-drink machine. Someone had put up a few pictures on the wall that were actually completed jigsaw puzzles over which an epoxy of sorts had been poured and allowed to dry to make them into solid pieces of down-home art, giving the room a rather cozy, thrown-together feel.

You could find me in this comfy hideaway every day on my fifteen-minute break in the morning and then again in the afternoon. Like most any teacher's lounge, people would come in for a few minutes between classes to catch up on what was going on. I thought of it fondly as the school's well-lived-in family room.

Sometime in late fall, I was sitting alone on one of the couches during my morning break, vegetating. The door popped open, and a young white man about nineteen years old, dressed in an official delivery uniform for Coke, burst in with his hand dolly stacked with cases of Coke bottles. The name embroidered neatly on his uniform was "Oscar," and he had come to replenish the machine. As he looked around, his eyes immediately connected with mine. I smiled and said hi. Looking at me, he froze in mid-movement. I thought maybe he hadn't heard me, so I repeated my cheerful greeting.

After a few more uncomfortable moments of silence, he set the front wheels of his dolly down but continued to stare at me. I rolled my eyes from side to side to see if I was missing anything, but no one else was in the room, and everything appeared just fine. It seemed to be turning into a weird encounter. Finally, in a rich, rural drawl, he loudly demanded, "Wha' y'all doin' here?"

Now I was confused, but I politely responded, "I'm a teacher here. Why?" Several more silent moments passed. *What's his problem?* I wondered. I finally said, "Oscar, just do your job and fill up the Coke machine. We've all been waiting for you to come, and we're glad you're here." So Oscar collected himself, turned away from me, and set about his job of replenishing the machine without a word.

As he left, I still hadn't figured out what had discombobulated him, so I simply said goodbye. He made no comment, just wheeled his cart of empty bottles out the door, shaking his head with a perplexed look on his face.

After putting the pieces together in my mind sometime later, I realized what Oscar's meltdown was all about—he couldn't make sense of my white face in a place that he thought of as entirely black. How had I ended up where I didn't belong? Didn't I know I wasn't supposed to be there? I was really messing with his otherwise very tidy racial boundaries. His world was a bit out of kilter because of my presence in that room. Later I wished I'd had the insight to tell poor Oscar that the world was changing, and he needed to get over it! But hindsight is always so much clearer, isn't it?

The world was changing for me, too. But I was happy with the revolution. I liked my teaching job, and I liked my new community.

I liked going to church each Sunday at Faith, and I liked the collection of new friends that came with all these different life experiences. I especially liked everything about this funny place called St. Elmo; it made me feel safe and accepted. I felt each day as if I was exactly where I was supposed to be, doing exactly what I had been created to do, as if I was in a welcoming sanctuary.

And the kids kept amazing me with their indomitable spirit. Each day, they seemed to arrive with a tenacity for wanting to improve their lives somehow. Daily, Antowan would greet me with his sunny smile and the words, "Hey, miss, wha' ya gunna learn me today?"

Life at this remarkable place was always full of great energy, and was anything but dull. Each day, I was caught up in creative ideas, trying to support educational opportunities for kids. One of the most prominent of these was the fund-raising ventures that kept popping up unexpectedly around the building. These efforts, organized by different teachers and staff, focused on the simple goal of raising funds for classroom books, equipment, and instructional materials.

One of these ventures was organized by my friend Jannel, the business teacher from across the hall. Once or twice a week, she would bring in hot dogs steeped in sauerkraut in a slow cooker. Then she would warm up the concoction and sell the stuff at lunchtime. Along with the sheer popularity of hot dogs as a noon meal, I was always impressed with the well-thought-out marketing strategy of including sauerkraut. At about eleven o'clock or so in the morning, when Jannel would turn on the slow cooker, the strong conspicuous odor of sauerkraut would leisurely waft across the hall and creep under the door into my classroom. Then everyone in my classroom would lose focus thinking about the hot dogs swimming in warm sauerkraut close by. At this point, any classroom activities would morph into discussions about how hungry we all were. The powerful odor of sauerkraut certainly was not lost on anyone in the general vicinity who was the least bit hungry and who had thirty-five cents in their pocket, and

Jannel would be a small step closer to another new typewriter for her classroom.

I loved the hot dogs and sauerkraut, so as the school year went along, I became a regular customer for Jannel. I would usually buy extra sauerkraut dogs for my students who didn't have lunch on a particular day. What great times we shared eating the food treasures together.

Never before or since have I experienced such free-market activity in a school environment. It seemed to be classic unfettered capitalism. Because school instructional funds from the district and state were essentially nonexistent, absolutely nothing was available for simple instructional equipment found in most any other high school, such as typewriters, microscopes, and overhead projectors, to name just a few. So these pop-up sales events organized by teachers and completely funded out of the teachers' own pockets were extremely common. I soon realized this free-market activity provided another strata of learning opportunity for students, as they demonstrated how to earn a bit of cash from whatever you could think of to sell legally. Although student-organized fund-raising ventures were never allowed, these staff-organized enterprises were valuable models for kids from dire economic circumstances. And without a doubt, the kids at St. Elmo were truly from dire economic circumstances.

So at lunchtime, the hot-dog-and-sauerkraut food table continued raising money for typewriters in the business classroom. The cookie table in the hall outside the gymnasium raised money for band instruments, the Kool-Aid-pops table in the hall adjacent to the cafeteria raised money for library books, and the chicken pie table in Mr. Harris's math class raised money for new math texts. These ventures around the school seemed to only be limited by lack of imagination.

I remember vividly a day in November when, after more than three years of hawking doughnuts at lunchtime, the science teachers had finally come up with enough money to purchase the high school's first microscope. When the prized piece of scientific equipment actually arrived on campus, celebrations began in the two science rooms, and then, like a wild river, excitement flowed throughout the school. I had no idea at first what was happening, but I was soon filled in about the wonderful news by a student who was going from classroom to classroom. It occurred to me that one microscope for a school of over six hundred kids meant time would have to be judicially rationed for democratic student use. But the good news, at least, was that the instrument could be the start of important learning opportunities. The bittersweet part of the story was that, because of the nature of the learning hierarchy in school, my special-ed kids were the lowest priority, not that I honestly believed a microscope would make much of a difference in instructional planning for my class anyway.

On that memorable day, the science teachers did allow anybody at the school who wanted to use the cherished microscope to line up and take a turn looking at a slide. In my class, I did the best I could to try to explain what a microscope was and what it could do. Then I said that whoever wanted to look through the new magical instrument should line up at the door. Every one of my students had been caught in the excitement of the morning and voluntarily stepped up, even though they had little or no concept of what a microscope was. Pauline enthusiastically helped with the organization of the short trip down the hall to the science classroom, directing who should be standing where in the line. Antowan, never one to take direction from Pauline, stood outside the classroom that held the microscope, hawking the upcoming opportunity as if he were a huckster on a carnival midway. "Come and see it!" he shouted, unable to pronounce the word "microscope" yet. But his excitement was contagious, and his skill at winning people over to what he was selling was on display for everyone. It wasn't just the microscope that was out there for people to see; Antowan was in his element doing what he did so well, captivating people—special-ed designation or not.

Just being able to have the kids see the microscope, and have each one look through it, added enormously to a positive classroom outlook. Although they would never have the instrument integrated into their learning plan, my kids had seen it and experienced it, and I thought that was pretty good, all things considered.

Unfortunately, technically explaining what the microscope was used for seemed to be an exercise in futility for me. All basic science concepts were pretty much lost on most of the students, despite my best efforts. Feelings of inadequacy as a teacher continued to overwhelm me. I believed that these students deserved so much more than I was able to deliver, but learning to celebrate small victories kept me getting out of bed each morning.

CHAPTER TWENTY-SIX

Baby Milner

Toward the end of January, I began feeling nauseated each morning and soon discovered that what I had been suspecting was true—I was pregnant. Although unplanned, the news was certainly not unwelcome. I had always hoped for a child someday, but I had not honestly contemplated the possibility since Ned's arrest. When the doctor confirmed the news, I was apprehensive of how a baby might impact our life, considering we'd had targets on our backs ever since the arrest. I had, after a good deal of angst, agreed to stay long-term in Mobile, and over the weeks and months, I had really come to understand the tenuous position in which we had found ourselves living.

All this swirled through my mind after the doctor's visit to confirm the pregnancy. I drove over to the University of South Alabama to pick up Ned from a Saturday-morning class. When he got in the car, I told him I had some important news. Then I told him what the doctor had confirmed that morning: he was to be a father if all went well. My predictable Ned, who always dealt with things from his head and not his heart, was slow in responding, as though he was taking in the stunning news of the possibility of

World War III. He seemed much more ambivalent about the idea of a baby coming into our lives than I was. The concept of a baby left him almost inarticulate, and clearly not openly excited. There were no smiles, no exclamations of joy.

His reaction crushed a long-held girlhood dream of mine. I had always seen this announcement happening with a tender embrace and kiss surrounded with loving, excited chatter. My moment was not marked with a tender embrace, kiss, nor any happy chatter. It was quite the opposite. Ned was aloof and uncommunicative.

The news did, however, put a whole new lens on our future plans. And this was what I think precipitated Ned's general lack of enthusiasm over the pregnancy. It struck me immediately that our current situation was not conducive to bringing a baby into our family. I was sure we both were still on the Klan's "Wanted List," and, needless to say, I didn't like the idea of bringing a baby into that kind of potential powder-keg setting. After all, it had been only six months since the arrest. Feelings across the Mobile community at large against Ned and what he had done were still very raw. It certainly would not have been impossible to figure out where we lived and worked if someone was consumed in hatred enough to do so. I found myself thinking about this possibility often, wondering when that trigger point might be realized in some vengeful mind.

So, for me, I began strategizing. The baby was due in late August, and by then I wanted to be reestablished in a place where I could feel more personal safety. We also needed more financial security. I wanted to be a stay-at-home mom, at least in the beginning years, so I didn't want to go back to work right away after the baby arrived. As it now stood, Ned's part-time job with an anti-poverty project in Mobile was not promising for the long term. And even if his part-time job was to continue, the income was not enough to support three of us. We both knew that by the end of the school year we would have to plan for major changes in our lives, which was quite distressing for my husband.

After a bit, though, Ned began trying to get on board with the idea of a move. Over the following few weeks, he sent out resumes to different anti-poverty and civil rights groups. At one point, there was interest from the American Friends Service Committee (AFSC), a Quaker organization that focuses on peace and social-justice issues in the United States and internationally. I was uneasy about this potential job offer, as this activist group was always on the cutting edge of civil rights situations, and AFSC workers were often putting their lives at risk furthering goals of the civil rights movement while living in the middle of some raging social cauldron. The difference between my husband and me was clear: because of the baby, I wanted to take a break from active daily involvement where I continually felt uneasy for our personal safety, and Ned wanted to remain in the thick of everything.

Unfortunately, I found Ned's point of view very difficult to argue with morally, but nevertheless, I felt an overwhelming need for us to figure out a plan for a safer life. And Ned felt we should just continue as we were without changing course in any way. He would not acknowledge my sense of fear, because, by not talking about it, the problem didn't exist. So we muddled along in this festering mess, each of us building up defenses to make sense of our position. And the most difficult part of it was that I had enormous guilt over my side of the argument. I secretly felt that my position, pulled from the morass of my fear quotient, was, in reality, morally indefensible. But I stubbornly stuck to my guns. And over time, Ned began to reluctantly take steps to passively move toward my wish of relocating.

Ned was finishing up his course work at the University of South Alabama. When he graduated in June, he would officially earn a BS in education. Teaching would then be an option, so he started interviewing with school district headhunters from around the country. A representative from the Cleveland Public Schools interviewed Ned and offered him a position as a high school science teacher.

To my relief, Ned accepted the offer to begin in September. He told me we could plan to relocate back to northern Ohio in early summer. Part of me was extraordinarily relieved, and I eagerly looked forward to being with my extended family when the new baby arrived. But part of me was stuck in guilt. The idea of leaving the place where I believed we had been a small but important part of the effort to try to change things for the better left me feeling like a sellout and, at times, downright cowardly. Our emotional struggle went on below the surface, even though it appeared to most people around us that we had come to a resolution. Despite having accepted the Cleveland job offer, though, a large part of Ned still wanted to figure out a way to stay in Mobile.

CHAPTER TWENTY-SEVEN

End-of-School Wrap

In May, as the school year was coming to an end, the heat and mugginess index was topping out. Ned had begrudgingly settled with me on a plan to pack our belongings and move back to northern Ohio after his graduation. But there was another graduation on the calendar first, the graduation at St. Elmo High School.

At school, I learned about a faculty picnic that was always held before graduation at a park by the scenic Dog River. Scheduled for a Saturday morning, the potluck was a rare opportunity to relax with teachers and staff without the time constraints of the school day. During the year, conversations had always been limited by school agendas and the need to fit life around car-pool requirements, leaving little time to really talk in depth with my colleagues. Further complicating social relationships was the fact that the St. Elmo faculty lived scattered throughout a wide area of Mobile County, and some teachers even lived across the state line in Mississippi.

Most of the faculty members showed up at the Dog River Park with their spouses, and after my husband's initial refusal to attend church with me recently and his lack of enthusiasm over the baby,

I was happy Ned was willing to go. I never knew what to expect from him since he'd resigned from the ministry. He was completely consumed in his own world of radical activities promoting justice, and I felt as though I were little more than an outside observer looking in at his life. At first the church community had given me a legitimate place in his universe, but now that he was a freelancer, so to speak, I felt I was left scrambling to figure out where I belonged, if at all.

The picnic tables were piled with platters of yummy-looking potato salad, fried chicken, summer fruit, and melon. I brought one of my dependable dishes, my mother-in-law's bean salad, and took some kidding on my "Yankee dish." Apparently, my recipe wasn't all that common in this coastal community, and anything different that came from me was labeled "Yankee."

My friend Jannel and I sat down on a bench, happy to finally have the chance to talk without demanding kids intruding. She introduced me to her husband, Moses, a tall, nice-looking young man in his midtwenties, dressed in ill-fitting, well-worn clothes. He said he worked in the hauling business. I wasn't sure exactly what that meant, but it seemed the work brought in very little income for the family. And since this was the revolutionary 1960s, with great credit due to the feminist movement, Jannel felt empowered enough to work outside of the home at a job that brought in a far better and more reliable income than a traditional house cleaner would make. A classic beauty in her midtwenties, Jannel had lovely round dark eyes and a wide, engaging smile. Born and raised in the nearby community of Theodore, the couple now lived with her two small children and her mother in the same small house Jannel had grown up in. The all-too-common narrative of unbelievable economic struggle came tumbling out again as Jannel talked about how hard it had been for her mother, who had little more than a second-grade education, to raise four children—especially after her father had died of a lingering illness. Both Jannel and Moses had attended completely segregated schools their entire lives, and teaching at St. Elmo had been a life goal for Jannel. A scholarship to Tuskegee Institute from the AME church was an enormous game changer for Jannel, and it ultimately resulted in her job as a teacher. She was a hard-working, proud product of the system and was now an essential part of the structure itself. And so some of the missing pieces of my friend's life had finally come together for me.

My car-pool friend, Clemmie, joined us, and the conversation moved to civil rights topics. Clemmie was especially pleased that Ned had come to the picnic. She and most everyone else there were taken by his reputation in local movement causes, and she was happy to be able to have some time to talk to him.

As the conversation refocused to Ned, I didn't feel like I wanted to share any of the personal tensions between us. This was because of my abiding sense of guilt. I didn't like to have my thoughts about leaving Mobile discussed with others, especially in a setting where Ned was considered the champion of the day. After all, we were soon going to move because of my worries. I was the person responsible for pulling away the man who stood for so much in their eyes. It was as though I was saying to them, *You all are not important enough for me to take risks and make sacrifices in my life. I want to leave here and go where I feel I can provide a safer life for my new child.*

So although I did discuss some nonpersonal details about our plans, I didn't talk at all about the tension this move was causing in our relationship. Secretly, I felt really overwhelmed with remorse as I saw myself responsible for our new direction, which would take Ned away from the area. The situation left me feeling alone, isolated from just about everyone, which was a damper on the good cheer floating about over the baby.

Ned enjoyed the picnic as he relished basking in the light of his public persona. It was no surprise this community continued to see him as a widely acclaimed local hero. The past ten months had done little to lessen this phenomenon. He was in his element with groups of people wanting to talk to him and thank him for his bravery. Although we had, of course, come to the picnic together, once we'd arrived, Ned never really connected with me personally in any way at all, including such things as eye contact, a smile, or a physical touch. This casual, aloof behavior toward me in public was not unusual, and it only reinforced my notion that I held little value in his life. Nonetheless, I was conflicted between pride in my husband and remorse over being the reason for us soon to be leaving Mobile.

•••

The day before graduation was the last official day of school, and almost all the students in my class showed up to celebrate the end of the school year. After thinking a lot about what would be a good way to say goodbye, I decided to give each one something that might have some meaning for them. I ended up making home-designed cards, each one personalized with simple printed statements, which included their name, like "Pauline, you are one of the best students ever" and "Antowan, thank you for being such a happy person."

As a special treat, I brought lunch for the kids—turkey sandwiches, chips, fruit, cookies, and lemonade. We spent the morning taking our last alligator outing, and in the afternoon we played simple games. There was no alligator to be found on the hunt that day, but the walk was filled with the sweet fragrance of newly minted summer flowers, and much silliness and laughter over the end of the school year.

I never learned the official names of flowers or any of the plants from my students. But despite this lack of scientific information, the world of the walks was a place where intriguing sights, sounds, and smells regularly greeted us. The cultural baggage each of us brought to the classroom mostly seemed to disappear at the door when we left the school to go on a hunt. Once outside in the humid, swampy environment, we were encircled in a sense of trust we found in that mysterious space. And I can assure you this comforting sense of trust appeared to extend to even the most disabled and disheartened among us. It was always a truly magical experience.

Listening to students add to the party-like aura with funny chatter on our last walk was a joy. I remembered only a few months before when I'd first met these emotionally awkward, silently withdrawn kids. If nothing else had been accomplished over the past several months, at least these endearing teens had learned to accept a strange-acting, and strange-speaking, woman—a "foreigner," as I remembered them calling me. I considered this acceptance to be the major accomplishment of the school year both for them—and for me.

A down side to this good memory was that I wasn't sure many of the kids even understood it would be our last day together. The concept of time, both future and past, was a troubling challenge for some to make sense of consistently. Antowan did understand in his own way, though. He told me he was "doin' some work down at the harbor" and wouldn't be back to school anymore. With that comment, I understood he would be another casualty of the economic-necessity war, which was always stealing opportunities from marginalized members of the community.

As the students left the room for the last time, I put my arms around each one at the door and held them close for a bit. I felt I wanted to say so much to each one, but I could only blurt out comments like how important they were to me and that they must take good care of themselves. Sweet smiles were shared in return as they walked out of my life. Smiles that made me acutely aware I was edging toward the end of my extraordinary journey in Mobile—a very bittersweet thought indeed.

•••

The next day was graduation. Well over two-thirds of potential high school graduates at St. Elmo had dropped out before graduation. These numbers were made up of the kids who had been blessed with the requisite IQs needed to complete all graduation requirements. But because of compelling financial needs of these kids' families, they had been pulled away from school and sent out to try to find work.

On the other hand, nobody kept track of special-ed student dropout rates. Kids with learning deficits would never earn a high school diploma, even if they had a family willing to let them stay in school for four years. There was no second-tier high school diploma they could aspire to like a certificate of attendance or some other legitimate diploma-like award at the end of four years. There really was no clear positive educational end point to school for them. So the act of quitting school to help their families around the house, or to find menial jobs, was an ultimate family expectation, like Antowan's story about finding work at the harbor.

Considering this piece of the puzzle, it was a wonder special-ed class attendance was consistently as good as it had been over the course of the school year. My job as a caseworker for the welfare department had made me very aware of the typical home environment of most, if not all, of these kids. The home visits I regularly made as a caseworker were still vivid in my memory, and I completely understood the conflict between education and the extraordinary need to help provide necessities. For these families, stark poverty was a debilitating disease demonstrated by symptoms of hopelessness and despair eroding deeply into the soul of each home. Job one was to merely survive—a day at a time. The possible benefits education might bring offered little hope when weighed against constant specters of hunger and maintaining a roof over your head.

It goes without saying, then, that high school graduation for those blessed with families able to afford it and for students with the intellect to earn it became an overwhelmingly gigantic achievement. Because so many teens had been weeded out of the educational process in the prior four years, the graduation event itself took on the aura of an enormous community celebration overflowing with hope and joy. In many ways, the occasion paralleled a deeply emotional Sunday-morning worship service with its depth of feeling.

Charlie Drum had come to our house sometime in April on official business as school principal to invite Ned to attend the graduation. Charlie believed that having Ned there would make several families of the graduates happy, including many of the graduates themselves, who considered Ned a remarkably brave man. Needless to say, Ned was delighted and agreed right away.

When graduation day at St. Elmo arrived, all faculty members were required to attend, and I wouldn't have missed it anyway. Because of the limited size of the multipurpose room used for graduation, the only teens allowed to attend were the band kids and, of course, the graduates. The rest of the limited seating space was devoted to friends and family of the graduates, along with faculty and staff.

I wore my best dress, a sleeveless turquoise silk shift with a stand-up collar. The loose, straight style was comfortable enough around the middle to look fine despite the minimal baby bump. The dark-blue high-heeled shoes were uncomfortable, as pregnancy had caused my usually narrow feet to swell each day, but I had no other choice. But I felt like I looked as good as I could, considering the circumstances.

Ned put on his dark-gray suit with a black shirt and his clergy collar, and he appeared at the school around midmorning. I had gone earlier with the car-pool gang, and as he entered the room, I thought he really did look quite dashing. I walked over and squeezed his hand. He smiled at me briefly and then looked away to find Charlie Drum. The nondescript room, giving off fleeting whiffs of Lysol, had taken on an air of festivity with a sprinkling of blue and white balloons. Rather wobbly, well-used folding chairs were lined up in neat rows with the end seats in the front two rows set off by large, puffy blue plastic bows. One main aisle down the middle of the rows neatly divided the room in half. I could clearly sense an energy that was hard to describe but that instilled the room with a rather awesome feeling of anticipation.

In the front of the room, adjacent to the cafeteria counter, was a line of five chairs facing the rest of the room behind a beleaguered-looking small wooden podium. And diagonally across a front corner about fifteen chairs were clustered in a group where the band was to sit.

Guests dressed in what was clearly their Sunday best quickly filled the room. Along with colorful flowered dresses, a few women wore large, showy hats and even gloves. While most men donned denim overalls and clean, well-worn cotton shirts, two or three wore some form of outdated dress suits with a shirt and tie and thin, tightly buckled belts. It was certainly an occasion to be marked with everyone's finest attire and best behavior.

The fifteen or so band members were bedecked in old, ill-fitting black-and-silver high school band uniforms with tall, stiff hats. These had been donated when another school had purchased new uniforms. St. Elmo band kids had never owned new uniforms. Each band member proudly held a thoroughly well-used band instrument. I had not seen the band in uniform, or even the instruments, in the nine months I had been at St. Elmo, so this image was a surprise to me. Over the months I had been teaching, I would occasionally hear what sounded like bits and pieces of band music drifting through the halls, but I had never paid much attention to it, and I certainly had not heard a piece ever played through.

The band lined up to go down the center aisle, followed by the faculty and then the graduates. With everything ready to start, the band director, Mr. Smallwood, stood in front of his trusty crew of student musicians and started to wave his baton. Then the band began to play. At first, an odd thought popped into my head: Had we interrupted a practice session of the band? And then I realized it was not practice at all but, indeed, the real thing.

As it turned out, the St. Elmo band's rendition of the traditional *Pomp and Circumstance* graduation theme was nothing if not memorable. What we all heard was the best attempt of kids of poverty with no real access to formal music lessons playing very old, cast-off instruments that had been donated after living out their best years elsewhere. So the end result was a performance that arose out of great dignity and dedicated effort, if not of fine technical accomplishment. And that was certainly enough for all of us.

As the band continued to play, they took their place in the front corner of the room, and the faculty lined up to march in ahead of the graduates. Faculty men were dressed in suits and ties, and the women wore nice store-bought dresses that fit the occasion.

Behind the faculty, the graduates lined up. Each of the thirty or so wore a long dark-blue robe zipped up the front and a conventional mortarboard hat with a gold tassel. All the trappings of what would be considered a traditional high school graduation most any place in the United States had been attended to by the planners of this event, except that around the edges, one could detect clear signs of extreme poverty. What might have been missing in fine, expensive accouterments such as expansive, over-the-top decorations, dependable band instruments, formal flower arrangements, and the like was made up for in a loving community spirit of make-do accomplishment and pride.

I felt a sense of humbleness walking in with the other faculty members. Just nine months before, these remarkable people of St. Elmo High School had welcomed me and made me feel a part of their community family when I was at one of the lowest points in my life. I had felt lovingly accepted into their carefully guarded black society despite my whiteness and all my silly Northern cultural baggage. They had incorporated me into their lives every day, and they never faltered in giving me the sense of being watched over and cared for. They truly had my back. What a profound experience this had been for me. And now I was included as an equal player in this grand year-end celebration.

After we marched in and took our places in seats behind the marked-off rows, the graduates came slowly walking, some almost strutting, down the aisle accompanied by loud clapping and cheering. Then Charlie began the ceremony by giving the usual welcoming remarks and introducing the graduate who would lead us in the Pledge of Allegiance. Things were bubbling along when, at one point, Charlie found a good place to respectfully introduce Ned, "the white man who cared enough to put his life on the line for us." I had not been prepared for that, but then I don't know why it surprised me; after all, Charlie had invited Ned. Long, loud applause, and even some cheers, could be heard as Ned stood up and waved to the group. His heroic reputation had not dwindled over the months.

Charlie did not connect the dots between Ned and me, the only other white face in the audience. And that was fine. As far as I was concerned, Ned was the hero; I was not. In fact, I was really beginning to see myself as the antihero, the reason being that Ned was soon to be leaving the area because of my wishes. I began to realize guilt had begun to replace fear as my best friend. What a depressing thought that was.

But I was also experiencing a sense of excitement underneath the guilt, excitement at the promise of my return to what I considered to be a more secure life in the community of my loving family in northern Ohio.

•••

The last day of work at St. Elmo was pupil-free. The day was scheduled to allow for teachers and staff to wrap up things in the classrooms in order to close the school for the summer.

I had been told there would be a faculty meeting in the multi-purpose room at eleven, so at about ten fifty, I got myself over to the faculty lounge, which was devoid of people. Sliding comfortably down into the couch cushions, I put my feet up on the little coffee table and thought to myself that there was absolutely no need for me to go to the faculty meeting since I wouldn't be returning the next year. I was feeling a little weary and thought I'd just hang out there on the couch until the meeting was over. At eleven, Charlie's voice came over the loudspeaker system announcing that all teachers were to report to the multipurpose room for the meeting. I just smiled and thought, surely, I wasn't included in that directive. I'd spent the whole year trying to do exactly what everyone had expected me to do at St. Elmo, and now I was just going to kick back and do what I wanted to do—sit there by myself and vegetate for a while. It was a luxurious feeling.

About eleven ten or so, Charlie's voice again came on the loud-speaker, and he repeated the directive for all teachers to report to the multipurpose room for the meeting. I smiled again to myself as I thought some folks were taking their sweet time to get to the meeting. I began speculating in my brain who that might be—the science teacher, Mr. Harris, or maybe even my friend Jannel. It didn't really matter to me, though, and I just giggled and stretched out my legs to be more comfortable, thinking again that the directive did not apply to me.

Finally, at about eleven fifteen, after one last directive on the loudspeaker for all teachers to please report to the multipurpose room, the door of the faculty lounge flew open. Standing there in front of me was Jannel with a funny look on her face. "Wha' ya-all doin here?" she demanded loudly with one hand on her hip the other waving wildly in the air at me. "Ya-all are supposed to be at the teachers' meeting." I sat up straight with a jerk and told her I had decided to skip the meeting since I wasn't planning to be back the next year. I told her I really didn't see any need to go. But my flimsy excuse fell on deaf ears.

Jannel told me to get my "sorry self" up off the couch and "hot-foot it over to the faculty meeting right away." Well, needless to say, I moved with great speed and followed Jannel down the hall-way in a half walk, half run, about two steps behind her. No fur-ther words were exchanged between us.

As I walked into the multipurpose room, I was greeted with shouts of "surprise" by loud voices. The place had been brightly decorated with crepe paper and balloons. A big sign said "Congratulations, Mrs. Milner." I was taken aback. It wasn't a faculty meeting at all but a surprise baby shower for me. I felt completely silly, and yet I was enormously pleased.

The faculty and staff had arranged a lovely assortment of gaily wrapped baby gifts along with a yummy potluck lunch. What a memorable time we had giggling over baby jokes and laughing over how I'd sat in the empty faculty lounge like a simpleton while they'd waited for me in the multipurpose room. Opening the generous collection of baby gifts was wonderful. But the gift I treasured the longest was the farewell card people had lovingly signed that read: "We think you are worth your weight in gold." The sentiment made the extra baby weight doubly acceptable to me.

So on my last day at St. Elmo High School, I was feted as a respected colleague who was appreciated entirely for her own work. I was beginning to understand I had no need to be attached to someone's coattails to matter; I was fine just the way I was. And I saw that realization as the school's ultimate gift to me.

CHAPTER TWENTY-EIGHT

Heading North

The thought of packing up three years of accumulated living into one U-Haul truck at first didn't seem to be that big of a deal. As time went by, though, the task became colossal. In addition to the truck, we had two cars, the Pontiac Tempest and the Opel. Ned's first thought was he would attach the Tempest to the back of the U-Haul and tow it behind the truck to Cleveland. The longer that vision lived in his head, though, the less he liked it. My husband was gutsy, but this crazy idea of driving a large truck while towing a midsize car behind it was beyond the pale for him. So we moved on to plan B.

Plan B provided for me driving the Opel and Ned driving the truck with our excitable Dalmatian, Tallulah, in the front seat next to him, leaving the Tempest behind for the time being. We thought that maybe we could come back over the Thanksgiving holiday and pick it up. This seemed like a far better plan in the long run.

Our good friends Judy and Arnie showed up early to help on the day of the move. They had staunchly been there for us throughout the astonishing challenges we'd faced over the past three years, and the fact that it was moving day didn't lessen their willingness to help.

Larger furniture pieces got put in the truck first, all the while giving careful thought to what might be the best way to protect things from sliding around. After we had loaded about a third of the truck, Herbert Madder and another neighbor from across the street, Melvin Brown, came over. Luckily, they had experience working for a moving company. Looking over our work, they explained to us that what we had done so far should really be undone. Essentially, we needed to start over, and they stepped up to help. As the day went along, they gave us great professional moving tips, like not setting furniture pieces on fragile legs but instead laying things on their side. By the time we had finished, things in the truck seemed remarkably secure for the long road trip ahead, and we were grateful to Melvin and Herbert and all the others who had helped. Late in the afternoon, we told the neighbors who had gathered outside by the truck how appreciative we were to the community for taking us in as they had. Then we shared our loving goodbyes and pulled out of the driveway for the last time.

It had been a long day, and we spent the night at Judy and Arnie's house before starting out the next morning. My head was spinning with all the moving stuff when, the next morning, we finally had to say goodbye to these two remarkable friends.

Driving off early that morning we wove our way through the old historic downtown streets of Mobile. Thoughts of the night we had first arrived late in the summer of 1966 began to roll over me. In fact, the memories became so overwhelming at one point that I almost felt I had to brush them from my eyes in order to see the road in front of me. This section of Mobile had always captured my imagination because of its quintessential Southern charm, where massive live oak trees held reign over the city.

The complicated life Ned and I had experienced over the last three years now all seemed like a strange elusive dream suspended and intertwined among the tangled web of Spanish moss overhead. I felt as though I were almost burying this whole astonishing time in the historic Church Street Graveyard I had just driven past.

Then, when the elegant trees and city buildings began to disappear, and open fields came into sight, the surreal feelings disappeared. It was hard to believe, but we were finally on our way north to our first night's stop near Nashville. The excitement I was feeling, about what was to come, filled the car with healing energy. With the windows rolled down, I breathed in the fresh air of rural south-central Alabama, all the while keeping a close eye on the U-Haul truck racing down the two-lane highway ahead of me.

Late in the afternoon of the second day, a sign that said "Elyria—22 Miles" popped into view, and I took in a huge breath of relief. We had made it. Both my mom and dad came rushing out of the front door, overjoyed, as we pulled into the driveway. I felt a sense of great peace.

We spent the next several hours relaxing and soaking up happy vibes with my parents. They were living temporarily in a wonderful old home outside of town on the banks of the capricious Black River. My mom listened intently to my chattering and was especially interested in the stories of teaching at St. Elmo. Ned and my dad talked about Ned's plans to teach at Glenville High School and about where he thought we might like to live.

I shared a bit of the arrest narrative with my parents and thankfully didn't feel any anger from them over how things had gone down for Ned, even though my dad was an ardent law-and-order conservative. His love for me, and acceptance of Ned, was evident, and we felt good being able to talk about our story without experiencing any heavy-handed judgmental comments from him. My parents encouraged us to stay as long as we wanted, but after a few wonderful days in Elyria, we knew we needed to drive to Cleveland where Ned's parents lived. Reconnecting with Ned's family would mean we would be taking a measure of how we now stood in their eyes after all the dust had settled on the saga of Ned's arrest. To be sure, neither one of us looked forward to that scene at all.

CHAPTER TWENTY-NINE

Life with
Mary and G. E.

The next day, we drove east twenty miles along the south shore of Lake Erie to Cleveland after leaving our sweet dog, Tallulah, with my parents in Elyria. Ned's parents lived in an upscale apartment building with a view of Lake Erie. They had talked with the leasing company about the possibility of Ned and I renting a small apartment in the building on a short-term basis while we looked for a more permanent home. This plan turned out to be a good solution for us, and we ended up renting a furnished apartment there for about six weeks, leaving Tallulah with our belongings in storage in the garage of Ned's aunt and uncle.

Ned's mother was guardedly happy when she first saw us, and his dad began with some light welcome banter. Ned's mother always waited for Ned's dad to dictate the correct emotional reaction to any situation, and that day was no different. It didn't take long for Ned's dad to turn the conversation to matters regarding Ned's arrest, though.

This was an awkward direction for us. I knew without question that both Ned's dad and my dad were not open to supporting anything to do with civil rights issues. They believed unequivocally that these "rabble-rousers," as they had dubbed civil rights protesters, deserved whatever trouble they found themselves in; although, in the past, Ned's dad had been quick to point out that he certainly didn't see himself as racist or anything. Both of our dads believed the civil rights movement was edging America too far to the political left, and therefore, the movement was surely connected in some demonic way to that familiar scapegoat, Communism. Both fathers would slap a Communist label on things they didn't like politically and let it wallow in legitimate disdain. And that's how I believed they truly viewed Ned's civil rights activities.

So when Ned's dad asked me in a surprised tone why I hadn't called him the night of Ned's arrest when I thought I needed to find bail, I said to him as politely as I could, "I'm not sure why I would have called you when I know how you feel about civil rights workers. You must know Ned was—and is—a true-blue activist. I'm really sorry, but the thought of calling you never entered my head." The truth of the matter was that I hadn't thought of calling either set of parents on that infamous night; although, in retrospect, I'm sure if I had called my dad, he would have helped me work something out.

My father-in-law took my response as a slap in the face. He often tried to act the role of beguiling model father; that's why he'd asked the question, but it was only for effect. He wanted to show how concerned he was—superficially. It had been a year since the arrest. And although he had been aware of Ned's protest actions since shortly after they had happened, he had never once called me to extend an offer of help. But now that we were face-to-face, he believed his inquiry alone made him seem concerned.

After my response didn't support the portrait of loving parent he was trying to conjure up, he awkwardly backpedaled, and soon after he exited the room for the shelter of his secluded, tiny den surrounded by his TV, books, and carefully selected family pictures—none of which, by the way, included me. And that was the end of any discussion of our Mobile experiences with Ned's parents.

I was quite pleased when Ned's dad retreated to his den. I found no pleasure in the traditional family pastime of sitting for hours listening to my father-in-law narcissistically dominate the conversation. As he sucked all the fresh air out of the room, he effectively polluted the confined space with his nauseating cigarette and pipe smoke. So his reluctance to engage with us any further about Mobile was perfectly fine as far as I was concerned. As for Ned, confrontations with his dad caused him to withdraw behind a great wall of silence that shut everyone out. It was clear that Ned, too, valued the prospect of not having to continue the discussion.

Ned's dad, known to various family members as G. E., George Edgar, or Uncle George, was an uncomplicated man. He viewed everyone as a potential devoted George Edgar Milner disciple. He would bully you with extraordinary temper tantrums to get you on his side, or schmooze or bribe you with things such as meals at expensive restaurants if, in return, you became his adoring supporter. The unspoken understanding was that you must sit for hours and listen to G. E. expound pretentiously on sports or politics or history or one of his never-completed works of romantic historic fiction.

Fancying himself a budding writer, G. E. would go on at length detailing the historical settings of his fantasy stories, always portraying himself as the—thinly veiled—handsome, dashing hero of each tale. Relevant comments were never welcomed. If you overstepped his limits by speaking out during his soliloquies—especially unfavorably—you would lose your membership to his fragile, self-absorbed universe. He would then sulk away to the safe confines of his miniscule den.

Ned's dad had successfully estranged himself from almost everyone in the extended family. It should surprise no one, then, that there were actually only two loyal family members left in G. E.'s world worthy of having their pictures displayed in his den—Mary, his wife and Ned's mother, and a favorite niece. On rare occasions, Ned might be included temporarily in this select group, because Ned did more than his fair share of silently soaking up the lengthy, self-absorbed rants. Ned's passive behavior always made me wonder what was going on with my otherwise outspoken husband.

At first, I was a little hurt by my exclusion from the picture display in G. E.'s den. He considered himself quite a connoisseur of great-looking women, and he perceived his gift to spot them as one of a myriad of his cultured and sophisticated talents. Apparently, he had decided that I didn't make the cut. It would seem I wasn't attractive enough to compete for space next to the photos of Ned's mother taken from a newspaper ad, where her photo had been used as a model for an aunt's hair salon, and the compelling pictures of the niece, who was about my age and beautiful enough to work as a professional model for major department stores, and who seemed to dote on her "favorite uncle George." It took a while for me to learn that my looks had not nearly as much to do with my exclusion as my unacceptably independent way of relating to him did. But the obvious act of exclusion was always evident to anyone who was daring enough to enter the inner sanctum of G. E.'s den. And after his only grandchild, my beautiful daughter, was born, he also omitted any images of her, I would guess because of her unacceptable mother—me.

Appearance was extremely important to G. E., and he would dress in outfits that looked like they had been pulled from the closet of the *Great Gatsby* cast—classy sports jackets, expensive-looking slacks, perfectly polished dress shoes, and even a cravat, all of which made him peculiarly overdressed in almost every situation. This fact probably didn't occur to him; however, if it did, I'm sure he would have relished the notion that he was sophisticated enough to show everyone else up. There was a small imperfection in the picture, though. G. E. was one of those men who had trouble finding the specific place on his midsection to place his belt. His short, thin, boney frame offered few body contours to give him any clues in his search, so his belt buckle was often a bit askew, sheepishly hiding under his sporty jacket. The odd angle of the belt buckle would often cause me to wonder if that flaw was maybe a hint that the interior of this Dapper Dandy persona wasn't as well put together as the exterior. His outlandish conceit included impeccably groomed, short, thinning gray-black hair and a pert little gray mustache that perched prestigiously on his sallow upper lip. His dark eyes would dart about the room swiftly as his body moved in quick, exaggerated, often clumsy flourishes.

While G. E. carefully crafted his behavior to appear as a cheerful, caring, and generous person, it was always a manipulation used to increase the number of loyal members in his self-absorbed universe.

Further, my father-in-law was continually trying to demonstrate for others what a caring husband he was, but the sincerity of this image was officially dispelled for me one afternoon when I unexpectedly dropped by the apartment. I was casually chatting with Ned's mother while Ned's dad—secretly, I guess—was listening from his adjacent den. I don't even remember what the conversation was about, but it was something quite innocuous, I'm sure. Well into our conversation, G. E. called Ned's mom into his den. He had apparently taken exception to some remark she had made, and he told her that he was enraged. I heard her begging him not to be angry as she started to cry. Then I heard the sharp crack as his hand hit her face. To say I was stunned wouldn't express my feelings strongly enough. She continued begging for his forgiveness as she sobbed. I was shocked by the violence and couldn't believe what I was hearing. But, intuitively, I knew any interference from me would result in him taking his fury out on her even longer after I was gone, so I just left. I felt awful that I hadn't tried to protect my victimized mother-in-law, but I didn't know how to do so without causing further retribution.

Although I told Ned about this heart-wrenching scene, he didn't comment on it or ever want to discuss it with me in the future. In fact, he would almost never discuss his father's behavior with me. When we spent time with his parents in their apartment, Ned always went along passively with his dad's dominant social behavior, following his mother's lead. This was the one family issue that bothered me more than anything else. Neither Ned nor his mother ever acted like there was anything at all disturbing about G. E. I couldn't figure out why they never challenged his disgustingly obnoxious behavior.

I would sometimes even wonder if there was something wrong with me because I found my father-in-law's actions so oppressive. Of the three of us, I was the only adult who seemed to find G.E.'s antics troubling. I soon discovered that holidays spent with Ned and our new daughter, Megan, in my in-laws' small apartment were next to intolerable. In order to survive, I resorted to long walks with Megan right after the meal. The outings provided a double blessing: not only was I able to avoid my father-in-law's boorish behavior, but I was also able to keep my young child out of the revolting, smoke-filled confines of the small space. By the time my daughter and I returned, Ned's dad had always retired to his den, where he would stay until Ned, Megan, and I left. The less my father-in-law had to do with Megan, the happier he was. The simple truth was he always saw Megan as major competition for attention—like he had when Ned was young. And G. E. was all about extinguishing any and all rivalry to secure the center-stage spotlight.

Again and again, Ned's aunts shared stories from Ned's childhood with me, revealing G. E.'s need to diminish Ned whenever and however he could. These stories would always be repeated quietly, as though, if told from behind a raised hand, I would understand they were family secrets that needed to remain hidden in the shadows. Somehow, these aunts—his mother's sisters—believed I should be entrusted with these disturbing tales. As troubling as this was to me—being the younger generation's trusted dark-secret-keeper—I did find the narratives to be unquestionable proof that George Edgar Milner would not tolerate any opposition for being the absolute center of everyone's focus.

A deeper look into G. E.'s charged personality showed that he always took great pleasure in showing off what he considered to be his unquestionable sense of moral superiority. G. E.'s final break with his family came when the Baptist minister of the family's powerful church apparently behaved in a morally inappropriate manner, and the church fired him. G. E. thought the minister should have been given more slack, I guess. So my father-in-law decided it was time to officially detach himself from his deeply integrated family interests, both in business and in church. It was a wild, midlife thumbing-of-his-nose at all things his extended family held dear.

Ned was fifteen at the time and had lived his whole life with his parents in a small unit on the same property behind his grandparents' house. True to what he considered his morally heroic stand in defending the pastor, Ned's dad decided to reinvent his life, removing himself from all extended-family interaction as a dramatic protest. He moved his small family to a chic new apartment twenty-five miles away on the shores of Lake Erie, finding a wonderful sense of who he really was by inventing a dashing new lifestyle. To top off this image, he pasted together a shiny set of slightly different religious beliefs, and joined a grand, rather elitist Lutheran church in the prestigious suburb of Cleveland Heights. Leaving his secure job as a salesman at the family business, Milner Electric, he went out on his own to become a successful salesman of electrical products.

But having a fifteen-year-old son hanging around in his exciting life was a problem for the new-and-improved George Edgar Milner. He believed that too much attention was being directed toward his son, and away from him, and that it finally had to change. He believed he had a thrilling life ahead of him, and his son, Ned, was in his way. So Ned's dad sent his fifteen-year-old son off to a military boarding school in Tennessee and never welcomed him back to live at home for any length of time ever again. The family would later pass it off as a good decision for Ned. Even Ned confirmed to me years after our marriage that the military school banishment was the best thing that had happened to him as a kid, because he was finally away from a life controlled by his father's violent tyranny.

By banishing his son, Ned's dad put the final touches on the grand new picture of himself—a comfortably well-off, sophisticated, and urbane man of the world. He loved the idea of debonair apartment life with a person at the front desk twenty-four seven and "the nice Negro man," as he referred to the garage worker, looking after his car in the ostentatious garage. George Edgar could even hobnob with neighbors like Bob Lemon, famous Cleveland Indians baseball pitcher, in his new digs. There was no need to think about investing in a home; although, they had never owned their own home and never would. G. E. believed life was so some much more gentile as an apartment dweller. One didn't have to trouble oneself with home maintenance and upkeep; one could just be the splendid gentleman with all the external needs of living attended to by others. Ned's dad believed he had truly "arrived."

Ned's mother, Marie Magdalene—or Mary, as she was known—was the youngest of six children born to devout German Mennonite immigrant parents and adored by her brother and four older sisters. Life had been difficult for the Hege family. There had always been a huge struggle just to keep a roof over the family's head. After high school, one of her sisters, a registered nurse, paid for her to attend one year of college—an unusual accomplishment for a woman during that time. In college, Mary had upgraded the cultural apparel of the Mennonites for a much more contemporary wardrobe and hair style, and pictures from that time show her to be an attractive modern-looking young lady. After funds ran out for school, Mary returned home. Through involvement in Baptist church–related events—as Mennonite groups were few and far between—she quickly met George Edgar Milner, and marriage soon followed.

It was no secret to anyone that Mary had "married well." The Milners were well-off and doing better year by year as their wholesale electrical business—Milner Electric—flourished in downtown Cleveland.

Mary became the dutiful wife, then mother, and finally loving caretaker for her ailing mother-in-law for the last several years of her mother-in-law's life. Living in Chagrin Falls in a house owned by her in-laws put her job performance under a constant microscope, and she apparently didn't disappoint the onlookers. But when, after several years, Ned's dad decided to leave the family social fabric and reinvent himself, Mary went along with no resistance. G. E. and Ned were her life. And when George Edgar sent Ned away to boarding school, she never uttered a negative word about the decision. As usual, she felt the overwhelming need to always defend anything and everything G. E. said and did.

This impressive picture of fine apartment living continued for several years. Ned's mother didn't drive due to her limited eyesight, so she was left alone for long periods of time in the apartment building, and she soon felt the need to have some additional outside interests in her life after Ned was sent away. Mary learned to take the bus and began to work as a volunteer at Lutheran Hospital in downtown Cleveland.

Before too long, she was hired for a newly created job at the hospital—director of volunteers. Talented, bright, and imbued with wonderful leadership skills, Mary contributed immensely to the life of the hospital in numerous creative ways over the next several years. Among other efforts, she was the major force behind the first Lutheran Hospital coffee shop, staffed with volunteers, which became a serious revenue stream for the hospital. She also envisioned and saw through to fruition the highly successful Garrett Shop, which took on the local Goodwill Industries in resale business, providing another solid source of funding for the hospital. Pretty much everything Mary Milner took on provided good outcomes for Lutheran Hospital, and she took on a great deal.

Coincidentally, in the early 1930s, Mary's father, Ulrich Hege, had worked as a hired hand on my grandfather's large farm in Wellington, Ohio. In fact, I have a treasured old faded photograph of my mother-in-law's father standing straight and tall next to my happy, handsome grandfather, Wesley Miller, taken about five years before my husband was born. Further, my aunt Hilda was named after one of my mother-in law's sisters—Hilda. The connections between Ned's family and mine were rock solid and went way, way back, and I think this family cement was part of what often kept me in my marriage during very stressful times. It seemed as though karma was at work.

In the late 1950s, about eight years into apartment life for G. E. and Mary, Ned found himself in the US Army stationed in Okinawa. After a good deal of introspection while living a life contrary to the values in which he had been raised, Ned lost much of his personal faith. Then, finally, following some deep soul-searching while living on that exotic island, eating food he had learned to love, immersed in a culture he held close, Ned discovered himself wanting a more satisfying relationship with God. And he began to believe he wanted to become a Christian minister.

When Ned returned to the states after his military service, he became strongly influenced by what he considered a bold decision his dad had made years earlier in becoming a Lutheran. Ned had loyally joined his mother in an undivided effort to defend G. E.'s religious choice of Lutheranism and thereby distance themselves from the rest of the Baptist-leaning Milner family.

What was not easy for me to follow was why Ned had aligned himself fairly effortlessly at this point in time with the Lutheran faith tradition as a starting point to begin theological studies. It seemed to me that Ned should have had a good deal of resentment toward his dad over how he had been raised, and would therefore have resisted his dad's religious choice of Lutheranism. But that was not the case. He was drawn into the religion by the influence of the charismatic pastor of his parents' church and before long came to the conclusion that he wanted to become a Lutheran minister—not Baptist. So he set off in the fall of 1961 to begin a four-year Lutheran seminary program in Springfield, Illinois.

By the time I came into the family in the mid-1960s, G. E. had been at times experiencing migraine headaches. Changes in technology, like the demise of the printed circuit, caused him to look for work in related fields, but these efforts became less and less reliable in providing a dependable income. So G. E.'s poor health and job challenges resulted in Ned's mother becoming the sole source of income for the couple. This situation continued for the last twenty-five years of their lives together. Mary's job at the hospital was her personal salvation in many ways, while allowing her to be the unfailing breadwinner for an extravagant spouse who was consumed by a heightened sense of entitlement.

Ned and his mother were always and forever G. E.'s foremost loyal cheerleaders. Although Ned's dad was never able to be fully at peace with the consequences of decisions he made that caused serious fractures with his extended family, he always remained the champion of the day, no matter what, to both Ned and his mother. But as the years passed, George Edgar became more and more isolated, and consumed with resentment. Ned's dad could never get past his belief that he had been socially ostracized and financially cheated by his father. From my first contact with Ned and his parents in 1964, this mantra of victimization always remained the prominent family theme for all three of them.

I believe this toxic narrative was the underlying cause of George Edgar's quite unhappy last few years. The dramatic business and religious decisions made years earlier did not result in G. E. becoming a stronger man who found inner peace. Rather, these decisions brought him a continuing sense of indignation. During the last few months of his life in 1967, long after Ned's parents had moved from their elegant lakefront apartment to a less ostentatious space, the old familiar Baptist faith of G. E.'s youth came creeping back into his psyche to haunt and reclaim his soul during the final days of his existence. The questions came back: *Did my decision to leave the Baptist church mess things up for me? Am I really saved? Have I done the right things so God will take me to heaven?*

As cancer tormented his body, the past tormented his soul. The drama of George Edgar Milner's search for independence did not have a storybook ending. And I am not particularly proud to admit that it's difficult to find the grace to see this man as a loving part of my life, even all these years later.

Up until Mary's own passing two decades after her husband's death, she remained blindly loyal to him by imitating his unloving, ungenerous spirit in her relationship to Ned, Megan, and me. It was as though any other behavior would dishonor G. E. in some way, even though he was gone. Family treasures and keepsakes—pretty much all she had left to her name—were given to friends, favorite nephews, and nameless retirement home employees over the years, not to us. She never seemed to want us to forget how really unlovable we all were, just as George Edgar had wanted us to believe. Although we were the main support in her life after his death, the powerful hold G. E. had on her right to the end was truly astonishing.

CHAPTER THIRTY

Coming Home

Despite my father's negative predisposition against civil rights activities, and his bias against the Lutheran faith tradition, he had, nonetheless, lovingly put all these feelings aside and generously offered to loan us money for a down payment on a house. His devotion to me clearly overcame his dislike of what Ned stood for. Since we knew Ned's teaching assignment would be at Glenville High School, we focused our house hunt on the east side of Cleveland and the surrounding communities. With my parents helping us with the down payment, and Ned qualifying for a VA loan, we were able to purchase a house.

On our limited budget, we were lucky to find a small, three-bedroom home in the fairly secluded East Cleveland community of Forest Hill. The place was located in a beautifully wooded chunk of real estate formerly purchased and developed by John D. Rockefeller Jr. on property that had been his boyhood home. Rockefeller interests had taken great care in preserving the land for future generations, so, in essence, a verdant wooded space had been gently transformed into charming residential neighborhoods with lovely curving streets and lush, tree-filled, parklike areas scattered throughout.

We settled on an older place situated on a tree-lined street of interesting homes. Each one had its own distinct personality. Ours—which would have been ranked number one on the street in terms of requiring basic renovations—was, in modern-day terms, a true fixer-upper. But we were delighted to be able to sign the papers and make it our own. We thought it was a wonderful find on our tight budget.

The baby was due the end of August. Everything seemed to fall into place fast with the house, and we were able to move in around the first of August, just in time to get a bit settled before the arrival of our new family member. Our neighbors, mostly retirees who had lived on the street for decades, were unusually kind and welcoming, and I felt at home almost at once.

My relationship with Ned had become much closer with all the activity a new home required. And to my great pleasure, Ned was showing surprising enthusiasm about the idea of the baby after all. He had taken a temporary job as a Pinkerton guard at a chemical factory over the summer until his teaching assignment started, so we thankfully had steady income to count on.

Our daughter, Megan Melissa, arrived the first week of September. She was healthy, happy, and full of great promise for a wonderful future. How blessed we were. What extraordinary joy this new little being brought into our lives. Since both my mother and my mother-in-law claimed they were "no good with infants," neither offered to come and help out when we arrived home from the hospital. So my devoted maternal grandparents arrived to help us care for our new little daughter.

Early each fall, the Little Brown Jug horse race is held in Delaware, Ohio. To my amazing grandpa Miller, this famous harness race was one of the highlights of his exciting year, and he would not consider missing it—except, it would seem, for the birth of a very adored great-granddaughter. So that year, he forfeited his prized trip to Delaware in favor of spending what turned out to be extraordinary family time with us in East Cleveland. Having my grandparents help us adjust to our new lives as parents was a gift I will never forget. It blessed our new family of three with deep love. But after a week of hand-holding, great home-cooked meals, and doting care, my adored grandma and grandpa Miller went back home to Wooster, and Ned and I were left with the demanding responsibilities of new parenthood all by ourselves.

Ned had just started his job teaching science at Glenville High School, and he seemed to be getting acclimated to his new career. My life had changed so dramatically as a new mom that I hardly knew who I was anymore.

Time bubbled along, and as we each settled into life on Hazel Road as new parents, it seemed that Ned began to feel a little left out because of the attention the new baby demanded. I wondered if his feelings were connected to the family life Ned had experienced as a child. After all, his father had always found it incredibly difficult to share the family stage with Ned, his only child. How much of Ned's reaction had been imprinted on him by his dad's behavior?

Additionally, Ned's work at Glenville High School didn't seem to give him much personal satisfaction. And thoughts of what he had left behind in Mobile continued to haunt him. These memories melted together in a pot already full of new baby demands. All this unhappiness bubbled under the surface and eventually turned for Ned into a growing sense of hostility toward me, the one he saw as responsible for his less-than-wonderful existence. The old frustrations over having to give up what he loved doing, which had come between us before, had not stayed in Mobile as I had hoped. Instead, these frustrations had surreptitiously followed us to Cleveland. Ned's behavior often became marked by long, angry episodes. Below all the huff and puff, I knew he felt as if he had made a bad decision in returning to Ohio. And that I was to blame for his stupid choice.

Since I felt completely responsible for the situation, I was often bogged down in bouts of depression. Taking care of a newborn didn't leave me much time to contemplate what was happening to our lives, but I knew our marriage was less than satisfactory to both of us. I was often in tears. Life in this glorious place I had wanted to think of as free from fear and unhappiness just wasn't as wonderful as I had anticipated. I was beaten up every day by the old adage: Be careful what you wish for.

Ned certainly didn't try to hide his resentment about the situation. He came to believe he could have, and should have, been doing something much more important for the civil rights movement than teaching at Glenville, and thanks to me, that goal had been thwarted. I was depressed because my expectations of a loving, supportive husband who doted on his new baby, and on me, were never realized. The upshot of all this dysfunction was having some pretty hollow feelings for each other.

I racked my muddled brain to try to figure out how I could change the situation I had caused. I tightly grasped scrappy bits of religious faith talk, like the Biblical promise that proclaims: "And we know that all things work together for good to them that love God." But being the impatient pessimist that I was, I sure wasn't seeing much in my life that was going to work out for good, even though I believed I sincerely loved God.

My favorite pastime, at first, was to lose myself in ethereal daydreams of a perfect, happy marriage. But it didn't take long for me to realize that effort was an absurd waste of time. The reality was a pretty pathetic new mother racked with guilt and depression. My basic faith principles were eroding. I was not someone a person might be excited to come home to after a hard day teaching high school kids, I'm sure. It seemed as though each of our demons brought out the worst in the other. Looking back on this period of time decades later, it's a wonder we made it through at all.

More than once, I considered leaving Ned—packing up my clothes and Megan's things and just walking out the door with my new baby in my arms. But where would I go? It wasn't right to ask my parents to take in Megan and me; they had already done so much, although I never doubted that they would have lovingly welcomed us. I didn't even have a car—something I had always provided for myself since college. We'd left Mobile with only one car, which Ned used each day for work. And the current family income could hardly be stretched to support two households if I did leave. I became preoccupied with the word "trapped." Its implications brought on great bouts of melancholy. My newfound sense of being a strong woman—independent and capable—was sorely tested.

The truth of the matter was that my pride was very much at stake. I had taken huge emotional strides away from the secure religious and political world that my family had defined for me growing up. Then, after connecting my life to Ned, I had often made what would have seemed to others—and probably actually were—pretentious pronouncements at family gatherings regarding my newly acquired social and religious beliefs. To up the ante, I always placed my vocal appreciation for my enlightened way of viewing the world on Ned—my moral and intellectual compass. I thought that admitting to the fact that I was now miserably unhappy in my personal relationship with my husband would demonstrate to my family how misguided and foolhardy I had been. I had bought into all that my dad would have called the "bleeding-heart liberal ideals" of civil rights causes and the scary new religious concepts Ned had promoted. So to my family and everyone else, I continued to portray Ned as the perfect husband by keeping our less-than-ideal relationship a secret. In my mind, if I let anyone know the truth of how unhappy I was, I would appear the fool. So I kept quiet and was an isolated, miserable mess.

Somehow it didn't occur to me that I could personally embrace my new social and religious beliefs while still admitting that things weren't going well in my marriage. That would have taken more insight and courage than I had in my emotional storage chest. Down deep, I liked my new way of seeing the world, and I held Ned close for having helped me unlock the doors to make it happen. I was such a neophyte at this new worldview, though, that I felt completely dependent on the person who had articulated and modeled these concepts to me. But my day-in, day-out existence with my husband was a sad one. Just holding on each day to the status quo was the best I could manage for the time being. Life for me was a troubling conundrum indeed.

CHAPTER THIRTY-ONE

Mobile Revisited

Amid all this emotional upheaval, Ned and I made plans to fly back to Mobile over the long Thanksgiving weekend to pick up our other car. While figuring out the logistics of the trip, it occurred to us that since we wanted Judy and Arnie to be Megan's godparents anyway, we might as well have our infant daughter baptized during our weekend in Mobile.

Although baptism of an infant is usually a big deal for most families, for us it was just the opposite. My parents' Baptist faith meant they did not value the idea of baptizing an infant, so not arranging our plans to include them seemed acceptable. And ironically, Ned's dad, the original family convert to Lutheranism and therefore the reason I had eventually acquired the notion of infant baptism to begin with, didn't much like the idea of attending a ceremony like a baptism where the baby took too much attention away from himself. So not including Ned's parents in baptism plans seemed like the best idea for that side of the family, too.

Besides, thinking about how my life had been transformed while living in Mobile helped me understand that having our baby daughter baptized there might possibly be a rather fitting end point to my Southern experience anyway. So arrangements were made for Megan's baptism ceremony to take place during the Thanksgiving-morning worship service at Arnie's church, Faith Lutheran, where both Ned and I were members anyway.

On Wednesday evening of Thanksgiving week, we boarded the plane to Mobile. We had made arrangements to stay with Aaron and Faye Michelson, a Mobile couple Ned had worked with in civil rights activities—both professors at the University of South Alabama. The couple had three small daughters and lived in a large home that could accommodate two extra adults and a new baby with relative ease, and we were grateful for their offer of hospitality.

Throughout my Baptist childhood, I had been taught that baptism was a voluntary act made by a mature person, precipitated by a "public profession of faith." The act of baptism was kind of like the frosting on the cake, if you will, assuring everyone that you had accepted Jesus as your Savior. It was a bit like saying now you had the *Good Housekeeping* seal of approval stamped on your Christian life because you had been immersed, or dunked, in the baptistery pool of the church. I believed that this public act sent the message that a person was in pretty good standing with the Almighty. You see, baptism was all about confirming the decision the person had made by accepting Jesus into their heart. And further confirming how that person was now right with God because of consenting to the act of baptism.

This concept of baptism was turned upside down for me in the Lutheran faith, however. In this belief tradition, the notion of infant baptism included the idea that baptismal water becomes God at work in the life of the infant, bestowing an extraordinary blessing of acceptance and welcome into the human family. Somehow, I very much liked the idea of seeing the action of baptism as celebrating God coming to us rather than us proclaiming that we had decided to come to God. After all, wasn't the concept of grace—or unmerited favor—all about God coming to us, undeserving souls that we are? Anyway, no matter how you sliced it, I loved the thought of my precious new child being blessed by baptismal waters, surrounded by dear and loving friends at the sacred altar of Arnie's church.

On that Thanksgiving morning, we popped out of bed after our late-night arrival, excited and ready to take on this mystical business of baptism. After a hurried breakfast, the Michelson tribe packed into their vehicle, following along after us in our old friend, the Pontiac Tempest. It felt good having the Michelson family supporting Ned, Megan, and me as extended family would do. It was quite poignant to have this group of loving humans, especially with their Jewish roots, want to join us on this odyssey, because it strengthened the notion of inclusiveness I was so wanting for this celebration.

Thinking about the previous three years of my life, I knew that my existence was now light-years away from where it had been in September 1966, when my husband and I had first arrived in this fateful place. Just two years before arriving in Mobile, I had been a Goldwater supporter, a political conservative and proud of it, just like my father. Controlled as I was by the religious fundamentalist voice in my head that declared all concern over social issues "of the devil," I had not done the daunting work of weighing issues with an open mind. Any curiosity I possessed had been buried in hateful indifference.

But the truth was that, underneath this religious fundamentalist voice, there had been another voice struggling to gain attention—a questioning voice demanding the right to be heard. During my late teens, this subversive voice had surprisingly encouraged me to take short trips to Oberlin College on my own to hear the likes of Pete Seeger and Joan Baez in concert, and even to sit in on a lecture by the remarkable Margaret Sanger. But, to be clear, the people in these Oberlin trips were seen as evil and not worthy of my time by my Baptist family. After all, the college I was attending, Baldwin–Wallace, was almost too much outside of the fundamentalist bubble for my family to abide, much less racing off to that radical hotbed, Oberlin College.

251

Slowly, though, this different voice seemed to push me into rather unthinkable territory. I had the audacity to marry a reckless, headstrong Lutheran pastor who took me off to the next chapter of my journey, Mobile, Alabama, where the real realigning of my worldview would take place.

After three years in Mobile, my belief system had undergone an unbelievable renovation. Amazingly, matters of justice and equality had become solid moral commitments for me. Additionally, my notion of God's love had become all-encompassing, not just reserved for the deserving few who had happened to say and do the right things religiously.

By experiencing what could only have been transforming grace in the midst of the lives of precious welfare recipients on the back roads of Mobile County . . . or standing in my kitchen listening to my neighbor adoringly thank my audacious husband—the man I had begun to think of as the enemy . . . or working with truly remarkable kids in that place called St. Elmo High School, I had been poked, prodded, and pushed into a new way of viewing life. All this felt like redemptive love at work for me. And the notion I had been raised to believe in, that redemption was a one-time, done-and-over thing in a person's life, was now replaced with a grander complexity. Startlingly, I learned that redemption is an ever ongoing process of wonderment. Who knew?

It should be no surprise, then, that the final wrap-up of this transformative three-year stint in Mobile was this spectacular event of our daughter's baptism. Celebrating a new existence through the miracle of baptism generated wondrous hope for the life of my beautiful baby daughter, as well as unfailing hope for my own future—truly grace at work.

Although I sure wasn't as in touch with all this then as I am now decades later, I did know on that warm Mobile Thanksgiving morning, November 1969, I had unspeakable reasons to be thankful. While commemorating the baptismal waters that brought a lifetime of sacred blessings to my new child, I found myself remembering with gratitude the extraordinary three years I had been privileged to witness and be a part of in Mobile.

Our dear, extraordinary friends, Arnie and Judy, met us at the church door that holiday morning. Among those there, also, were the black congregation members of Faith Lutheran Church, some friends from our days at Holy Cross Lutheran Church, and an assortment of friends from Ned's civil rights work who chose to witness the baptism of our daughter while celebrating the Thanksgiving holiday together. It was a wonderful coming together of people who had meant so much to us during our sojourn in Mobile.

And our infant daughter, Megan Melissa Milner, was the first white child to be baptized at Faith Lutheran Church in Mobile, Alabama. As a proud, official member of the church on that morning, I felt as though I had truly come home.

EPILOGUE

Ever since we left Mobile, Alabama, in 1969, I wanted to record our experience of those three fateful years somehow, in some way. The person responsible for this task was clear to me. My husband, Ned—the hero of the story—should be the one to do the job. I saw it as a legacy he owed our family. But the years went by, and despite my occasional suggestions, nothing happened on the husband-taking-responsibility front. Life always got in the way. And more importantly, Ned just didn't connect to the idea in the same way I did.

Through all the changes in our lives, the story vaguely hung around in the recesses of my mind like an old jacket I had tucked way back in our closet in the possibility that *someday* my husband would pull it out and wear it. Time went along, though, and nothing happened with the old jacket. It just continued to passively hang there.

But something did happen with me. The memory of the tale began to take on a life of its own, haunting my psyche. It was a first-rate apparition, rudely forcing itself toward the front of the line of my daily thoughts. Coupled with this distraction was the obvious and pressing idea that time was running out for the main actors in the drama—Ned and me—to tell about it firsthand.

The more I wandered about with this ghost plaguing my life, the more I started to think that maybe I should take on the job myself. Now, this was a tough transition to make because I had always seen myself as the unwitting bystander in the experience. I was, after all, the woman in the narrative—*not* the superstar man. For me, this deeply entrenched idea that the woman's place is secondary in a marriage relationship had been reason enough to think I should never take on the plan to write the story. After all, I hadn't even been a particularly cheerful player in the drama for much of the time anyway.

But somehow it came together a few years ago. I'd signed up for a writing class and was in a book group where two of the women had already written books themselves—all great subtle points of inspiration for me. And then one day I just decided to pull that old jacket out of the back of the closet and see how it would look on me instead of on my husband. I started putting some ideas down, and slowly but surely the goal evolved into me writing a "for real" book telling of our years in Mobile.

The story I had planned to write was still Ned's. Yes of course, that would be the plan because he was the hero. I struggled as I wrote. My filter kept getting in the way, and I had trouble not writing things as I—not Ned—had experienced them.

Terrie Silverman, the wizard of a writing coach in my class, encouraged me to lean into this impulse and relate *my* memories of what happened during that time—how *I* felt about the things that occurred. She gave me permission to see that my story was every bit as valid (and probably as interesting) as Ned's was. I was taken aback when presented with this notion. The opportunity to be as open as I could, and to tell about my shame and anger tempered with the redemptive love that I found in my life through all the turmoil in Mobile fueled my resolve to stick with writing the story.

The cherry at the top of the sundae came a few days ago when my superb production editor, Emilie Sandoz-Voyer, sent me some promotional copy for the book to look over. In the copy, a possible promo piece said, "As Molly became the hero of her own story . . ." and I had to gulp back my surprise. Here I am looking at the end of this book project thing—a miracle to be sure—and someone smart and competent, yes a very talented professional *woman*, had actually read what I wrote and thought I was a hero, too! Let me tell you, it just doesn't get any better than that for me.

Stories abound of people acting bravely while standing with the poor and oppressed. Hopefully this is one more small contribution to that integral body of literature. Ned and I have been graced to stand alongside all the courageous warriors in our narrative as well as all the bold men and women who have come before. And now, some fifty years later, I find myself relying on the strength I gained in writing and living this tale as the cause of the Resistance crosses my path each day. In the wisdom of Martin Luther King Jr., the effort to "redistribute the pain" continues, and by discovering my identity, I happily join the fray.

ACKNOWLEDGMENTS

My writing was enriched by historical recollections from Arnie Voigt, Judy Voigt, and, of course, my husband, Ned. My gratitude to them for their help is immense.

The cadre of caring women in my life that have supported me from the beginning of this journey are my own personal heroes—Marty Enold, Barbara von Mayrhauser, Gloria Cooper, Desi Casaus, Nada Ronning, Cheryl Anderson, and Ann Spier. Additional women in my life who have been incredible sources of inspiration for me are Lupe Reyes, Mary Nichols, Aryola Taylor, Carlynn Huddleston, Carolyn Herron, Pat Williams, Roberta Nathanson, Krimhilde Roth, and Pearl Baker. Their friendship has gifted me with confident assurance that I could write this narrative.

Technical writing help from Terrie Silverman has been invaluable. And the finished product is due to the superb professional assistance of the Girl Friday Production team, headed by my terrific production editor, Emilie Sandoz-Voyer. They held my hand tightly all the way through.

ABOUT THE AUTHOR

© *Megan Milner-Kutsch*

Molly Milner grew up in Elyria, Ohio, and has paid her dues as a caring pastor's wife in three different Lutheran congregations over forty years. She spent her career in mentorship and education, working as a high school teacher, GED program administrator, adult high school diploma coordinator, and as principal of a K–12 independent study school for the Los Angeles Unified School District. Now retired, she loves to travel, paint, and spend time each week with her strong and resilient grandson. She lives in Los Angeles with her husband, Ned, and her rescue standard poodle, Magnolia. This is her first book.

Made in the USA
San Bernardino, CA
29 May 2018